Christodao

"This book is pathbreaking. Professor Heup Young Kim brings together his decades-long studies in theology—East and West—to bear on the critical issues of our time. His profound knowledge of Christian theology as well as Confucian cosmology makes this book a unique contribution to interreligious dialogue. There are few people who have developed such an in-depth understanding of these traditions in the contemporary world. Professor Kim has written about and participated in dialogue between Christianity and Confucianism for decades. Indeed, this is a culmination of his trilogy of books on this topic beginning in 2017. His academic contributions do not end here, though. He brings his scholarship to bear on original reflections on the critical problems of environment and AI. He illustrates how a cosmological perspective infused with *qi* (matter-energy) provides a more inclusive worldview for care for our living earth community. Moreover, he provides a sophisticated perspective on the ethical challenges of AI in the global context. With its call for a Way of right resonance, this superb book will be a lasting contribution to our shared planetary future. Our gratitude is boundless!"

—MARY EVELYN TUCKER and JOHN GRIM, Co-Directors, Yale Forum on Religion and Ecology

"The incarnate Christ is an intensification of the cosmic rhythms. More than merely imitating Christ, we are invited to participate. That's Heup Young Kim's invitation to us."

—TED PETERS, Co-Editor, *Theology and Science*

"This book is beautifully crafted, with language so fresh it made me wonder: What might have happened if the first Christian theologians had engaged Eastern writers like Lao Tzu as well as Plato? Heup Young Kim's *Christodao* offers just such an engagement. It is the definitive statement of his lifelong project that bridges East and West and offers us a re-envisioned Christianity. If you share my weariness with the same old rationalistic dogmatics, I encourage you to let *Christodao* awaken your heart to a new world of possibilities."

—RON COLE-TURNER, Professor of Theology and Ethics Emeritus, Pittsburgh Theological Seminary

"East Asian Christianity has passed through many stages. Its earliest development saw it embedded in the cultural and philosophical context, but others have resisted and denied such inculturation. Professor Kim's work shows the maturity of the intercultural impulse, not simply finding resonances but reimagining what Christianity can mean in a world infused with Confucian, Daoist, and Buddhist sensibilities. Written accessibly, this book is also rich, deep, and profound and will reward repeated reading."

—Paul Hedges, Professor, S. Rajaratnam School of International Studies, Nanyang Technological University, Singapore

Christodao

The Way of Jesus, Trinity,
and Spirit in the Flow of Dao

Heup Young Kim

CASCADE *Books* • Eugene, Oregon

CHRISTODAO
The Way of Jesus, Trinity, and Spirit in the Flow of Dao

Cascade Books
An Imprint of Wipf and Stock Publishers
199 W. 8th Ave., Suite 3
Eugene, OR 97401

www.wipfandstock.com

PAPERBACK ISBN: 979-8-3852-6255-7
HARDCOVER ISBN: 979-8-3852-6256-4
EBOOK ISBN: 979-8-3852-6257-1

Cataloguing-in-Publication data:

Names: Kim, Hŭb-yŏng, 1949– [author].

Title: Christodao : the way of Jesus, Trinity, and Spirit in the flow of dao / Heup Young Kim.

Description: Eugene, OR: Cascade Books, 2026 | Includes bibliographical references.

Identifiers: ISBN 979-8-3852-6255-7 (paperback) | ISBN 979-8-3852-6256-4 (hardcover) | ISBN 979-8-3852-6257-1 (ebook)

Subjects: LCSH: Confucianism—Christian interpretations. | Christianity and other religions—Taoism. | Trinity. | Jesus Christ. | Holy Spirit. | Theology of religions (Christian theology). | Christian converts from Confucianism. | Christianity—East Asia.

Classification: BR128.T34 K56 2026 (print) | BR128.T34 (ebook)

Quotations from the *Dao De Jing* follow the Chinese original text, with reference to the translations of D. C. Lau (*Tao Te Ching*, New York: Penguin, 1963) and Wing-tsit Chan (*A Source Book in Chinese Philosophy*, Princeton University Press, 1963), occasionally modified by the author. Chapter numbers are indicated in parentheses in the text.

To teachers, companions, and fellow pilgrims on the Way.
(1 Cor 4:1–2)

Contents

List of Figures

Preface

Walking the Threefold Dao: Christ, Trinity, and Spirit in Rhythmic Harmony

THIS BOOK IS THE fruit of over three decades of theological labor, dialogical engagement, and spiritual listening. Building on the foundations laid in *Christ and the Tao* (2010), *A Theology of Dao* (2017), and *Theodao (Theology of Dao) II* (2025), this volume presents the most current expression of my Christodao vision, now expanded to include the further developed formulations of Trinitodao and Pneumatodao. Together, these offer a theological arc that spans Christ, the Trinity, and the Spirit, refracted through the prism of Dao.

Here, the Dao is not merely a philosophical backdrop but the structuring rhythm of divine reality—the flow through which Christian faith is re-voiced and re-walked in East Asian resonance. From Jesus as the embodied Way to the Trinity as relational harmony and to the Spirit as breath and return, this work offers not a systematic theology but a living theology, a rhythmic unfolding in resonance with the wisdom of heaven, earth, and humanity.

This volume also resonates with our time—a period of digital acceleration, artificial intelligence (AI), and planetary fragility. In this new era, theology must not only defend itself but also discern its own boundaries. Pneumatodao explores the Spirit's role in the Anthropocene, in an age shaped by algorithms and ecological rupture, and proposes *orthodao*—right resonance—as a renewed moral grammar.

In preparing this volume, I have intentionally reduced the number of footnotes and technical apparatus to make the work more accessible to a wider readership, especially those engaging with East–West theology, interreligious wisdom, or postcolonial cosmology. While rooted in academic reflection, it is written in the voice of invitation rather than assertion.

In addition, technical renderings of Hebrew and Greek have been provided in plain transliteration, while the original characters of Chinese and Korean have been omitted in favor of *pinyin* (for Chinese) and the Revised Romanization of Korean. This choice was made for the sake of readability and consistency, ensuring accessibility for readers who may not be familiar with original scripts.

In preparing this manuscript, I utilized the assistance of AI tools, specifically ChatGPT, to enhance clarity, rhythm, and editorial refinement. This was especially valuable as I write in English as a second language. While AI served as a responsive tool, the theological vision, interpretations, and final form of this work remain entirely my own responsibility.

To walk the Way is to breathe with it. My hope is that this book will not only help readers think differently, but also walk differently—in rhythm, with compassion, and in attunement with the Dao that never ceases to flow.

Heup Young Kim
Yeongju, Korea

Author's Reflection

Walking the Way in Yeongju

This book was written not in abstraction but in the rhythms of a place.

I wrote surrounded by the Sobaek Mountains of Yeongju, my hometown, a region long revered in Korean Daoic cosmology as a sacred range where heaven and earth whisper in mist.

To the north stands Buseoksa Temple, the cradle of Korean Huayan Buddhism, where the vision of interbeing has endured for over a millennium.

Nearby, to the East, is Sosu Seowon, the first private Confucian academy officially recognized by the state, where generations of Seonbi scholars cultivated sincerity, integrity, and reverence for the Way.

These are not merely historical monuments; they are living spaces of wisdom.

Both Buseoksa and Sosu Seowon are now UNESCO World Cultural Heritage Sites; not as relics of the past but as symbols of cultural continuity and contemplative life.

Together, they represent a triad: the Daoic Mountain, the Buddhist Temple, and the Confucian Academy. Here, I walk and write in the midst of their resonance.

I am a Christian theologian, but my spiritual roots are Confucian and Daoian. I come from a family shaped by a millennia-long tradition of rigorous Confucian living.

I am also a convert—called into the Jesus Way not by severing the past but by walking through it.

My conversion did not erase my formation; it reframed it.

The values of filial piety, moral cultivation, reverent silence, and cosmic relationality did not vanish in baptism—they found new breath.

Theodao, and its unfolding in Christodao, Trinitodao, and Pneumatodao, is not a theoretical exercise in interreligious synthesis.

It is the articulation of a lived resonance.

It arises from walking the pine paths of Sosu Seowon at dawn, from meditating in Buseoksa Temple, from wrestling with *han* (collective unresolved suffering), and from breathing the Spirit's wind through East Asian imagination.

It is theology born of pilgrimage—homeward and forward.

This is why the bibliography in the pages that follow is not merely a record of texts.

It is a map of conversations I have walked within, across cultures, languages, and spirits.

I do not stand above these currents. They have shaped me.

And so, I offer this work in the hope that it, too, may resonate—not as doctrine concluded but as a path still walked.

PART I

Christodao: The Embodied Dao

Part I introduces Christodao, a fresh vision of Jesus Christ reimagined through the dynamic, relational framework of East Asian thought. Here, Jesus is portrayed not merely as divine Logos or moral exemplar but as the living embodiment of Dao—the Way. Each chapter explores a different facet of Christ through Daoian[1] and Confucian lenses, presenting him as qi[2] (vital energy), Taiji[3] (harmonizer of

1. In this work, I distinguish between the terms *Daoist*, *Daoian*, and *Daoic*. In the Korean context, unlike in China, Daoism has historically been limited in its organizational structure as a religion; however, the term "Daoist" primarily connotes Daoism as a religious tradition. To avoid this restriction, I employ "*Daoian*" (parallel to "Confucian") to denote philosophical or cultural expressions rooted in Dao, and "*Daoic*" to refer more broadly to qualities and perspectives shaped by Dao, encompassing both Daoian and Confucian dimensions.

2. *Qi* is the Chinese term for vital energy, while *Ki* is its Korean and Japanese cognate. All three derive from the same classical East Asian cosmological notion of life-force or breath-energy that animates the cosmos and human existence. In this book, *qi* is used as the primary term for consistency, except in the case of *Sin-ki* (Korean), where the Korean form is retained. The wider cosmological and medical functions of *qi* are explored in Needham, *Science and Civilisation in China*, and its moral-spiritual dimensions in Confucian thought are examined in Tu, *Confucian Thought.*

3. *Taiji* (Korean: *Taegeuk*): the "Great Ultimate," the generative unity from which *yin-yang* emerges. In East Asian cosmology, *Taiji* represents dynamic relational balance rather than static substance. In Trinitodao, it serves as a symbol of God's unity-in-flow.

opposites), and Seonbi (Korean sage of compassion and integrity). This part proposes a holistic Christology deeply rooted in relational harmony, ecological interconnectedness, and embodied spirituality.

CHAPTER 1

In the Beginning Was the Dao: A Christodao Prologue

From Logos to Dao as the Walking Way

1.1 A Theological Threshold: From Logos to Dao

"In the beginning was the Word." So begins the majestic prologue of the Gospel of John. For centuries, this verse (John 1:1) has anchored Christian understandings of Christ's cosmic identity, affirming Jesus as the Logos—divine Word, reason, and ordering principle. In the Western theological tradition, Logos became the cornerstone of Christology, providing a metaphysical framework shaped by Greek philosophy, particularly the rationalist and essentialist currents of Stoicism and Platonism.

Yet when this verse was translated into East Asian languages—most notably Chinese, Korean, and Japanese—the term *Logos* did not become *Yan* (word) or *Li* (principle) but rather *Dao*, the Way. This was not a casual linguistic equivalence but a profound hermeneutical gesture: a recognition that *Dao*, in East Asian cosmology, resonated more fully with the dynamic, relational, and ineffable reality named in the Johannine Logos.

This translation of Logos as Dao thus opened a doorway to what I call *Christodao*, a third theological paradigm distinct from both the metaphysical *Logos* paradigm and the liberationist *praxis* paradigm. If Western theology has largely moved between *Theo-logy* (God-talk) and *Theo-praxis* (God-action), then East Asian theology today must press forward into *Theodao*, a theology of the Way.[1] And in doing so, we must reimagine Christology not merely as a doctrinal affirmation but as an invitation to walk the Way—ethically, cosmologically, relationally, and ecologically.

1.2 The Macro-Paradigm Shift: Christodao as Theological Renewal

The encounter between Christianity and East Asian thought dates back to the early Jesuit missions in China during the sixteenth and seventeenth centuries. Figures like Matteo Ricci (1552–1610) notably translated Christian concepts into Chinese philosophical language, employing terms such as *Tianzhu* (Heavenly Lord) and *Dao* to convey Christian understandings of God and Christ.[2]

In Korea, similar efforts emerged during the late Joseon period, when Confucian scholars engaged with Christian teachings, leading to vibrant theological and philosophical exchanges.[3] Building on these historical precedents, Christodao extends this intercultural dialogue—not as mere linguistic borrowing but as a hermeneutical engagement deeply rooted in the shared intellectual and spiritual heritage of East Asia and Christianity.

Root metaphors have shaped the historical development of Christian theology.[4] Western theology has long been dominated by what I call the Logos paradigm (*Theo-logy*) as a rational inquiry rooted in metaphysical abstraction. Western theologians from Justin Martyr to Thomas Aquinas constructed comprehensive systems of doctrine grounded in Greek conceptions of *Logos* as

1. See H. Kim, *Christ and the Tao*, 135–38; H. Kim, *Theology of Dao*, 14–18; H. Kim, *Theodao II*, 201–301.

2. See Standaert, *Chinese Voices in the Rites Controversy*, 19–25; Brockey, *Journey to the East*, 112–20.

3. See Baker, *Korean Spirituality*, 58–65.

4. See McFague, *Metaphysical Theology*, 13–29.

ratio, order, and universal reason.[5] This paradigm emphasized orthodoxy, propositional truth, and divine transcendence.

In the twentieth century, modern theologies, especially those arising from Latin America and postcolonial contexts, introduced the praxis paradigm (*Theo-praxis*), which emphasized history, justice, and the struggle of the oppressed. This liberationist turns made theology the interpretation of Christian commitment in action.[6] Yet even this corrective model remained tethered to the Western logic of history, dialectics, and linear political progress.

Both paradigms, I argued, share a foundational flaw. They remain trapped in *Western dualisms*—form and matter, spirit and body, theory and practice. They are insufficient to capture the holistic, dynamic, and cosmological vision of East Asian spirituality. What we need now is a third paradigm: a *Theodaoian macro-paradigm*, grounded not in Logos or praxis but in *Dao*.[7] This is not a mere metaphorical revision; it is a paradigmatic transformation of how theology begins, speaks, and moves. From this ground emerges *Christodao*—a Christology of Daoian–Confucian resonance, relational harmony, and cosmological communion.

1.3 Dao, Not as Concept but Way

To understand Christ through the lens of *Dao*, we must resist the temptation to treat Dao as a fixed concept or static category. As the opening line of the *Dao De Jing* warns: "The Dao that can be spoken is not the eternal Dao" (1).[8] Dao is not a "thing" or an abstract

5. See Justin Martyr, *First Apology*, chs. 5–6; Aquinas, *Summa Theologiae* 1.34.1.

6. See Gutiérrez, *Theology of Liberation*, 3–15.

7. For early versions of Christodao, see H. Kim, *Christ and the Tao*, 155–82; H. Kim, *Theology of Dao*, 34–56.

8. Laozi, *Dao De Jing*, ch. 1. Translations of the *Dao De Jing* follow the Chinese text, with references to Lau (*Lao Tzu: Tao Te Ching*) and Wing-tsit Chan (*Source Book in Chinese Philosophy*) and are occasionally modified by the author. References are cited in the text by chapter number, e.g., (*Dao De Jing* 40) or (40).

metaphysical essence but the ungraspable reality that underlies, pervades, and animates all things.[9]

In classical East Asian cosmology, Dao is the way reality flows—the relational patterning of the cosmos, the path of life, and the source of transformation. It is the movement of heaven and earth, the rhythm of *qi*, the creative principle of becoming, and the harmonizing energy that connects all beings in mutual resonance.[10]

This vision makes *Dao* both deeply compatible with, and profoundly different from, the Johannine *Logos*. Where *Logos*, in its Hellenistic reception, tends toward abstraction, transcendence, and hierarchical order, the *Dao* emphasizes immanence, rhythm, and relational harmony. Where *Logos* seeks to systematize truth, *Dao* invites participation in the mystery of life.

To confess that Jesus is *Dao* is to affirm that he is not merely the proclaimer of truth but the Way that is walked, the Truth that is lived, and the Life that flows in harmony with heaven and earth. In the Christodao vision, this is not a metaphorical flourish but a theological reorientation—an invitation to follow Christ as the living rhythm of creation, whose presence unites the divine, the human, and the cosmic in one continuous flow.

1.4 Christ and the Flow of *Sin-ki*: Introducing *Ugeumchi* Phenomenon

To deepen the vision of Christodao, we must draw on the profound East Asian intuition of *qi/ki*—the vital energy that pulses through all existence. In Korean cultural memory, poet-theologian Kim Chi-ha's (1941–2022) description of the *Ugeumchi phenomenon*[11]

9. See Laozi, *Dao De Jing*, chs. 14, 25.

10. See Zhuangzi, *Book of Master Zhuang*, ch. 6.

11. The *Ugeumchi* phenomenon refers to Kim Chi-ha's poetic description of fish leaping upstream in polluted waters, symbolizing how seemingly powerless creatures resonate with a hidden upward force, metaphorically representing the spiritual resistance and resilience of the marginalized, particularly highlighted during the Tonghak Revolution of 1894 in the Ugeumchi Hill.

offers a compelling parable of this life-energy and its theological significance.[12]

He recounts a scene from Haenam (a small city in southwestern Korea), where, in a polluted, rushing stream, small, weakened fish leap upstream against the torrential current. The miracle, he observes, is not found in muscular power but in resonance: the *Sin-ki*—spirit-energy—of the fish aligns with a hidden upward flow within the downward flood.[13] In that alignment, vitality and resistance converge.

This image serves as a theological parable for the Tonghak Revolution, when the Korean *minjung* (the oppressed people) rose up against foreign domination and systemic injustice. Even when crushed by the "cannons of empire" and the "demons of history," the *minjung* experienced an inner uprising of collective *Sin-ki*. It was not mere political willpower but a deep attunement to the life-giving current of heaven and earth.

From a Christodao perspective, Christ is not simply the metaphysical Logos or a political liberator but the incarnate resonance of Dao—the cosmic fish leaping against the stream in harmony with the unseen flow of divine vitality. Salvation, in this light, is not merely substitutionary atonement or juridical transaction; it is harmonization—an attunement to the cosmic rhythm of Dao that empowers even the broken and marginalized to rise.

The *Ugeumchi* phenomenon is not merely a sociopolitical memory but a *sociocosmic Christological motif*. It reveals salvation not primarily as substitution or juridical transaction, but as communal re-attunement to the cosmic rhythm of Dao—a *harmonization* that enables even the crushed and trampled to rise together.

12. See C. Kim, "*Ugeumchi* Phenomenon," 18–40.

13. *Sin-ki* literally means "spiritual energy" or "divine vital force." It denotes the dynamic interplay of *spirit* (*sin*) and *energy* (*ki*), signifying both the vitality of life and its radical return against distortion under collective sin. In Theodao, *Sin-ki* resonates with the work of the Spirit, healing alienated energies and restoring harmony.

1.5 From *Dabar* to Dao: Resonance Across Traditions

The Christodao vision also reframes the biblical roots of *Logos*. The Hebrew word *dabar*—translated as "word"—does not refer to an abstract principle but to a performative utterance, a word that enacts what it says. In the creation narrative of Genesis, *dabar* is the speech that makes being possible: "God said, 'Let there be light,' and there was light" (Gen 1:3–4).[14] In the Prophets, *dabar* is fire in the bones (Jer 20:9), a hammer shattering rock (Jer 23:29), and the breath that animates the dry bones of Israel (Ezek 37:4–10). It is as much action as it is speech.

In this sense, *dabar* is more akin to Dao than to Logos in its classical Greek philosophical meaning. Dao, like *dabar*, is living, generative, and relational. *Dabar* resonates with *qi*, just as Dao pulses with *Sin-ki*. Both name the dynamic, life-giving reality through which the cosmos is continually brought into harmony. When Jesus, as Logos, is re-rooted in *dabar*, he is no longer seen as the static essence of Greek ontology but as the living utterance of God—speech that moves, breathes, heals, calls, and walks among us.

To confess Jesus as "the Dao of *dabar*" is to recognize him as the one who embodies divine speech as flowing compassion, embodied resonance, and harmonizing grace. His life is not only the subject of doctrinal statements but a path of attunement. To follow him is to vibrate in harmony with the divine *qi/ki* that animates all creation.

1.6 Christ as *Hodos*: Walking the Way

In John 14:6, Jesus declares, "I am the Way, and the Truth, and the Life." The Greek term for "way" is *hodos*—a road, a path, a journey in motion. This is less a static doctrinal claim and more an existential invitation: *Walk with me. Follow my rhythm. Enter the flow.* Dao, too, is *hodos*. It is never a possession, never frozen into formula; it is always lived, always walked. The Dao is the unfolding

14. See Wenham, *Genesis 1–15*, 15–17.

path of life, traced not on maps but in the attunement of heart and action to the cosmic rhythm.

Jesus embodies this Daoic *hodos*. He does not hand down an abstract theory of salvation. Instead, he walks the dusty roads of Galilee, touches the bleeding woman (Mark 5:25–34), embraces the shamed (John 8:1–11), confronts the powerful with gentleness (Matt 23:1–12), and enters death with a non-coercive love. His life demonstrates *wu wei*—non-forcing, effortless action that nonetheless transforms the world.

The cross becomes the ultimate inversion of worldly power: *yin* overcoming *yang*, weakness revealing the deepest strength, harmony overcoming domination through the rhythm of Dao. Resurrection, in this light, is not merely proof of divinity but the restoration of cosmic balance—the return of heaven and earth, and all creation, to their original attunement in Dao. To say Jesus is the walking Dao is to confess that he harmonizes the world not by force but by becoming its rhythm. In him, the *hodos* and the Dao converge: the journey itself is the destination, and the Way is alive in the one who walks it.

1.7 Toward a Christodao Theology

Christodao is not simply an exercise in adding Daoian or Confucian language to an existing Christological framework. Rather, it represents a re-visioning of Jesus from within an East Asian cosmological imagination, where theology, ethics, and ecology are interwoven into a single theanthropocosmic fabric. In this vision:

1. *Metaphysical dualisms*—so deeply ingrained in the Logos paradigm—*are deconstructed.* Spirit and body, theory and practice, heaven and earth are no longer opposing categories but interdependent aspects of one harmonious whole.
2. *Political reductionisms*—often present in the praxis paradigm—*are transcended.* While liberation from oppression remains vital, it is understood within a broader cosmic harmony that includes all beings, not only human society.

3. Christology is reoriented within a *theanthropocosmic framework*, in which God, humanity, and creation exist in mutual resonance (*ganying*).[15] Salvation, then, is not merely juridical pardon but the healing of relationships and the restoration of cosmic attunement.

4. The wounded body of history—marked by colonization, injustice, and ecological devastation—is not redeemed through substitution alone but through *cosmic resonance* with the life-giving flow of Dao.

5. *Orthodao* replaces the binary of orthodoxy (right doctrine) and orthopraxis (right action) as the new grammar of Christian life, where "right way" implies right relationality, right balance, and right participation in the flow of life.

Such a Christology invites the church into *resonant discipleship*—a way of following Jesus in which belief is breath, theology is attunement, and justice flows from the deep harmonies of divine *qi*.

1.8 The Journey Ahead

Acknowledging potential critiques, Christodao is careful to avoid the trap of simplistic syncretism. Some may argue that interpreting the core doctrines of Christianity through the lenses of Daoian or Confucian wisdom risks diluting their theological integrity. However, as interreligious theologians have noted, authentic intercultural engagement—when pursued with methodological rigor and

15. *Ganying* (*Gameung* in Korean) is a classical East Asian concept literally meaning "resonance" or "sympathetic responsiveness." Originating in ancient East Asian thought—especially prominent in Daoism and Confucianism—*ganying* describes the subtle, dynamic connection by which all things in the universe respond to one another through invisible yet profound resonances. It denotes not only physical or emotional responses but also spiritual and ethical interconnectedness. In this book, *ganying* is employed as a theological metaphor and philosophical principle to articulate how divine reality (Dao, Spirit) intimately engages with humanity, nature, and even technology, highlighting a vision of existence as inherently relational and responsive.

a posture of deep respect can enrich rather than diminish religious identity.[16]

Such dialogue uncovers resonances that are not mere analogies but shared insights into the nature of ultimate reality and the way of life it entails. Christodao thus envisions dialogical *integrity*:

- It honors the distinctiveness of Christian confession—rooted in the incarnation, cross, and resurrection—while allowing these to be refracted through East Asian cosmological imagination.
- It affirms that theological truth is not static but dynamic, unfolding as the church encounters new cultural and historical horizons.
- It invites both critical discernment and spiritual openness, holding doctrinal fidelity and intercultural creativity in fruitful tension.

The chapters to follow unfold the Christodao vision through a series of thematic explorations:

- Christ and *Qi* (vital Spirit-energy)
- Christ as *Taiji*, the reconciler of opposites
- Jesus as *Seonbi*, the Korean sage of integrity and compassion
- The cross as cosmic resonance, and resurrection as return to Dao
- The church as a harmonizing community of responsive life

In the end, this is not a theology of abstract propositions but a theology of walking. Christ as Dao calls the church to live in the rhythm of divine *qi*, to leap like the feeble fish of the *Ugeumchi* parable—not by force but by aligning with the upward current hidden within the floods of history. To follow Christ is to flow in tune with the *Sin-ki* of creation, to walk the Way that is both ancient and ever new.

This is the Christodao—the Jesus who is the Way of Dao.

16. See Tracy, *Dialogue with the Other*, 58, 95.

CHAPTER 2

Christ in the Flow of *Qi*: A Christodao Pneumatology

Spirit-Breath, Sin-ki, and the Energetics of Salvation

2.1 Why *Qi*? Reframing Spirit Through Christodao

In the Christodao vision, Christ is not a remote metaphysical abstraction but the *living resonance* of Dao. If Dao is the dynamic Way of cosmic becoming, then *qi* is its animating rhythm—vital energy, breath, and relational Spirit that drives the process of becoming. Dao flows; *qi* pulses. In East Asian thought, *qi* is the subtle, all-pervading force that binds heaven, earth, and humanity into an indivisible continuum.

It is not merely "energy" in a physical or mechanistic sense but the sacramental vibrancy of life itself, the dynamic presence that courses through wind and breath, mountain and river, body and soul. As such, *qi* transcends the dualistic divisions between spirit and matter, the sacred and the secular, and the inner and outer life.

In the context of Christology, *qi* offers a *pneumatological grammar* for understanding Jesus not as an abstract divine essence defined in ontological categories but as the incarnate embodiment of *dynamic resonance*. Christ is the one in whom *qi* flows most fully, most harmoniously, and most redemptively. His life is the place where the rhythms of heaven and earth meet without friction, where the woundedness of creation is gathered into balance and restored. To speak of Jesus "in the flow of *qi*" is to situate him at the very heartbeat of the universe—restoring balance to all that has been fragmented by violence, hierarchy, and disconnection.

This approach reframes the meaning of the incarnation, not as a supernatural "interruption" of the created order but as its *perfect attunement*. Christ does not arrive to suspend the natural flow but to bring it to fullness, aligning human life with the original rhythm of Dao.

Qi Christology thus calls us beyond the logic of Western metaphysical substances and into the poetics of *energy, resonance, and harmony*. It represents a theological movement:

- from *being* to *becoming*;
- from *essence* to *flow*;
- from *explanation* to *attunement*.

In this sense, salvation is not merely a juridical pardon or a metaphysical transformation but the re-entry of human and cosmic life into the life-giving current of the Dao through the *qi* of Christ. This sacred energy—what the Korean tradition names *Sin-ki*—is the Spirit-energy that moves history upward through love, healing, and justice, even amidst oppression and decay.

2.2 *Qi* and the Spirit-Breath of Life

In classical East Asian texts—Daoian, Confucian, and medical—*qi* is described as the *breath that animates all things*, the relational energy that moves between heaven and earth. *Qi* circulates through channels in the human body just as it circulates through rivers and winds in the larger cosmos.[1] *Qi* is the pulse of life, the form of Spirit as breath, motion, and subtle influence.

This resonates deeply with the *biblical tradition of ruach* and *pneuma*. *Ruach* is the divine wind that hovers over the deep (Gen

1. See Veith, *Yellow Emperor's Classic*, 22–25.

1:2), breathes life into Adam (Gen 2:7), and animates the prophets. *Pneuma* is the Spirit who descends as a dove, as fire, and as wind; it is the indwelling life-force of the early Christian community (Acts 2). The Spirit is not a static doctrine but a dynamic event, much like *qi*.

Thus, we are not creating a false analogy but revealing an *ontological convergence*: Both *qi* and *pneuma* name the Spirit not as substance but as *relational vitality*—animating, connecting, healing. In the Christodao vision, Jesus is not the breaker of nature but its most resonant manifestation. His Spirit is not imposed upon creation but *flows from within it*, like *qi* flowing through meridians, like breath enlivening dry bones.

2.3 The Incarnation as Resonant Embodiment

Traditional Christologies often frame the incarnation in terms of *metaphysical descent*: God assumes human nature, adding substance to substance. This language—rooted in Greek philosophical categories—has served the church for centuries, yet it risks turning Jesus into a doctrinal puzzle rather than a relational presence. It can obscure the *rhythm* of embodiment in favor of an *ontological grammar*.

Qi Christology offers a different horizon. "*The Word became flesh*" (John 1:14) is not an act of inserting divine essence into human material but an event of *resonating fully with the flow of cosmic qi*. Jesus is the one whose life harmonized completely with the Dao, whose Spirit moved without obstruction. His being was not static but vibratory—an embodied channel of divine *Sin-ki* (Spirit-energy). In his words, his touch, his tears, and even his silences, Jesus became the resonant point where heaven and earth kissed.

As the *Ugeumchi* story suggests, such resonance is no mystical luxury but a *revolutionary power*.[2] Just as feeble fish leap upstream by uniting their *qi/ki* with the hidden *yin* currents, so Jesus moved upstream in history—resisting empire, healing trauma, and

2. See C. Kim, "*Ugeumchi* Phenomenon," 39–46.

restoring dignity—not through domination but through attunement.[3] His incarnation is a cosmic harmonization that empowers all life to find its own voice in the Dao. This vision reframes the incarnation away from metaphysical importation and toward a *mutual in-dwelling*: divine vitality inhabiting human life by perfect resonance. Christ's embodiment is thus not a suspension of nature's order but its fulfillment—the place where creation's deepest pulse is heard and magnified.

2.4 The Energetics of Healing: Christ's *Virtus* as *Sin-ki*

In the Gospels, healing emerges not as a display of theatrical command but as the overflow of *attuned presence*. In Mark 5:30, Jesus perceives that "*power (dynamis) has gone out from him*" when the bleeding woman touches his garment. Luke 6:19 tells us, "*Power came out from him and healed them all.*" Early Latin theology referred to this as *virtus*—efficacious energy, not coercive force.

This *virtus* finds a striking parallel in *qi*, which heals not by disruption but by restoring the *flow*. In Daoian and Confucian traditions, a sage is one who has cultivated inner *qi* to such harmony that their very presence becomes medicinal. Healing in this vision is not magic but resonance: Blocked energy is released, balance is restored, vitality returns.

In the Christodao perspective, Jesus' *qi*—his *Sin-ki*—was pure, unobstructed, and abundant. Out of this fullness, his presence restored what was blocked in others. He did not manipulate external forces; he allowed divine vitality to flow freely through his embodied life. To be healed by Christ is therefore to enter into his

3. Dolores Williams, who developed "Hagaritic theology," emphasizes that the central struggle for oppressed women is survival and the building of a "quality of life." This provides a model for resisting oppressive structures not through dominating power but through a transformative will to live, analogous to moving "upstream" through attunement with a deeper, life-giving current (*Sisters in the Wilderness*, 75–84). Pneumatodao similarly breathes through *han* (unresolved collective suffering)—not erasing it but honoring and transfiguring suffering into communal wisdom.

field of resonance—to have one's disordered *qi* realigned within the rhythm of Dao.

His compassion is not merely an emotion of pity but a *vibrational harmony* with those who suffer. His miracles are not violations of nature but nature's own completeness revealed: the cosmos resonating at its most whole.

2.5 *Sin-ki*, *Ugeumchi*, and the Energetics of Salvation

In the Christodao paradigm, *salvation* is not an escape from the world but the restoration of harmony within it. The *Ugeumchi* story—introduced in prior volumes—reminds us that *qi* is more than healing energy; it is *revolutionary vitality*.[4] In that tale, the feeble fish swim upstream because their *Sin-ki* aligns with the hidden upward currents within the flood. So too, the oppressed—*minjung*, crucified peoples, violated creation—rise not by overpowering but by resonating with the deeper pulse of divine justice.

In this vision, salvation is not a substitutionary transaction but a *collective realignment* with cosmic vitality. Christ becomes the archetypal fish in the flood, the fully resonant body of *Sin-ki*, where divine and historical *qi* converge.

Through his death and resurrection, Christ does not evade the cycle of suffering; he *transfigures it from within*, opening a path for all creation to leap again. This is not romantic mysticism but the *sociocosmic narrative of exploited life*: bodies broken by empire, souls crushed by hierarchy, lands poisoned by greed.[5] In Christ, these wounded realities are neither erased nor bypassed. They are *attuned*—restored to the deeper current of the Dao, awakened to their own vitality, and invited into *resonant communion* with the Source of life.

4. See H. Kim, *Christ and the Tao*, 138–48; H. Kim, *Theology of Dao*, 48–56.
5. See H. Kim, *Theology of Dao*, 29.

2.6 Toward Energy-Christology: Pneumato-Anthropocosmic Implications

A Christology of *qi* is, by its nature, a *theology of resonance*—a vision where life, Spirit, and cosmos form an indivisible whole. It resists the dualisms of Western metaphysics, which split spirit from matter, and it also resists the linear historicism of certain liberation theologies, which reduce salvation to a linear sequence of political events. Instead, *qi* Christology invites us into what may be called *pneumato-anthropocosmic communion*: the sacred harmony of Spirit (*qi*), humanity, and the entire created order.[6] Such a vision carries profound implications:

- *For ecological theology*, it frames Christ not as a distant redeemer detached from the earth but as the *rhythm of healing* pulsing within the biosphere itself. His saving work is a renewal of the planetary meridians—restoring flow where human greed has blocked life's currents.
- *For feminist and postcolonial theologies*, it shifts the focus away from hierarchical control toward embodied vitality, honoring the agency and dignity of marginalized bodies as bearers of Spirit-energy.
- *For interreligious dialogue*, it creates a bridge where Pneumatology can converse deeply with East Asian cosmology—neither diluting the uniqueness of Christ nor reducing Dao to a metaphor but offering mutual illumination.

In this framework, discipleship is not merely about moral conformity or intellectual assent. It is *attunement*—walking the Way, breathing with the Spirit, healing through presence. To follow Christ is to cultivate *Sin-ki*, to become a harmonizer in a world choked by dissonance, and to participate in the cosmic music of the Dao.

6. See H. Kim, *Theology of Dao*, 26–28.

2.7 Conclusion: Christ the Breath of the Way

Qi is not an abstraction. It is the breath we draw, the pulse we feel, the warmth we share. In Christ, this breath becomes articulate; this pulse takes form as a path; this warmth unfolds as the Way. Jesus is the *Christodao of qi*—the embodied resonance of God's life, restoring not only souls but the very fabric of being. His incarnation invites harmony, his death deepens our rhythm, and his resurrection reawakens the cosmic flow.

In a world fractured by domination and noise, Christ breathes a deeper rhythm. Those who are weary are called to inhale their life; the oppressed are summoned to rise like fish leaping in the rain-fed stream; creation itself exhales in relief.

The Way is not lost.

It is alive.

It flows.

CHAPTER 3

Jesus the Path: *Wu Wei*, *Kenosis*, and the Way That Walks

Non-Coercive Power and the Rhythm of Christ

3.1 Introduction: The Way That Walks

IN THE CHRISTODAO VISION, Christ is not first and foremost a concept to be affirmed or a creed to be recited but a Way to be walked. His identity, as revealed in John 14:6, "I am the Way, and the Truth, and the Life," does not privilege doctrinal truth over ethical path, or essence over encounter. Rather, it roots Christology in ancient intuition, shared across cultures, that truth is found not in grasping but in journeying.

To understand Jesus as *hodos* is to shift theology from proposition to pilgrimage, from metaphysics to motion. In this chapter, we deepen the Christodao perspective by reading Jesus through the rhythm of the Way, guided by the East Asian principle of *wu wei* (non-coercive action) and the Christian doctrine of *kenosis* (self-emptying love). Together, these traditions reveal a Christology of relational flow, in which Jesus enacts not power-over but power-through harmony.

This "Way that walks" naturally anticipates chapter 5's portrayal of Jesus as *Seonbi*, the Confucian scholar-sage, but it begins here with a reevaluation of Christ's own journey—his walking, yielding, healing, and embodying of Dao.

3.2 *Hodos*: The Pathway of Christ

In early Christian memory (e.g., Acts 9:2; 19:9; 22:4), Jesus' followers were not originally called "Christians" but members of "the Way" (*hodos*). The term in Greek denotes a road, path, or course of travel, connoting not static belief but lived direction. When Jesus declares, "I am the Way," he invites his disciples into a relational journey rather than a metaphysical category.

This shift—from *logos* to *hodos*—mirrors the Christodao transition from abstract formulation to embodied praxis. The Gospel of John, while rich in theological reflection, never separates belief from following. Jesus walks from Galilee to Jerusalem, meeting people along the way and disrupting social boundaries through his movements. In every encounter, his identity is disclosed not in isolation but in the unfolding of the Way.

Daoic cosmology shares this emphasis. The Dao is not primarily a system of propositional truths but a Way to be walked. "The Dao that can be spoken is not the eternal Dao" (*Dao De Jing* 1); the Way reveals itself only as one moves in attunement with it. Likewise, the Christian disciple does *not possess* Christ as doctrine but *follows* Christ as Way. To interpret Jesus as *hodos* is to honor the relational, dynamic, and ethical shape of his life. Christ is not merely the gate through which we enter salvation but the path we walk within it. In this sense, the Logos becomes *hodos*, and Christodao takes on ethical weight.

3.3 *Wu Wei*: The Rhythm of Relational Action

Daoic ethics are marked by one of the most misunderstood yet profound concepts in classical East Asian thought: *wu wei*. Often translated as "non-action," it is better rendered as "effortless action," "non-coercive doing," or "action in harmony with the Dao."[1] It is not passivity but a cultivated responsiveness that moves in resonance with the rhythms of life rather than imposing one's will upon them.

The sage does not act by force but by attunement. As the *Dao De Jing* observes: "The soft overcomes the hard; the yielding overcomes the rigid" (36, 78)—wisdom that turns conventional notions of strength upside down. *Wu wei* names the ethical posture of acting in alignment, not domination—responding to the world as a musician responds to a melody, or a dancer to the pull of gravity.

Christ's ministry embodies this principle at every turn. He refuses to wield coercive power, rejects domination, and teaches in parables that invite contemplation rather than demand submission. He yields to interruptions on his way (Mark 5:30), weeps with mourners instead of retaliating against enemies (John 11:35), and washes the feet of his disciples rather than assert hierarchical authority (John 13:5).

His miracles are not spectacular displays of force but gentle restorations of flow: healing hemorrhages, calming storms, loosening tongues, and raising the dead with a word, a touch, or a breath. His divine authority does not confront nature as an adversary; it moves with creation, bringing its rhythms into wholeness—*wu wei* flowing through suffering into restoration.

In the Christodao vision, Jesus as Dao walks in *wu wei*. His Way is one of soft strengths, quiet subversion, and radical humility. This reframes divine power not as sovereignty and control but as relational responsiveness and compassionate presence—a power that does not crush but restores.

3.4 *Kenosis*: Christ's Self-Emptying Dao

In Christian theology, *kenosis*—from the Greek word "to empty"—names the voluntary self-emptying of Christ in the incarnation and

1. See Slingerland, *Effortless Action*, 6–15.

crucifixion. As the hymn in Philippians 2:5–8 proclaims, Christ "did not regard equality with God as something to be exploited, but emptied himself, taking the form of a servant . . . and became obedient to the point of death—even death on a cross."

Traditionally, *kenosis* has been interpreted within metaphysical and moral frameworks: a relinquishing of divine privilege, a model of humility, or a pattern of redemptive suffering. But in the Christodao paradigm, *kenosis* becomes more than a moral example—it becomes ontological resonance with the Daoic flow of *wu wei.*

While *wu wei* and *kenosis* arise from different civilizational horizons, they converge in their ethical energy. Both signify noncoercive power; both value humility over assertion; both reveal a strength rooted not in domination but in vulnerability and alignment with a greater rhythm. Just as *wu wei* describes action that moves in harmony with the Dao, *kenosis* describes divine action that flows into creaturely form without resistance. It is not God abandoning divinity but God's life harmonizing itself with the vulnerable, finite rhythms of embodied existence. Christ does not "fall" from heaven as an alien power; he flows downward like rain, saturating the earth through surrender.

The *Dao De Jing* speaks in similar tones: "All streams flow to the sea because it is lower than they are. Humility gives it its power" (66). This image finds theological fulfillment in the downward movement of Christ's life: born in a manger, walking the roads of Galilee, touching people with leprosy, eating with outcasts, yielding to arrest, embracing the cross. Here is *kenosis* in Daoic rhythm—power revealed in yielding, glory disclosed in descent, victory manifested in love's vulnerability. In Christodao terms, this self-emptying is not the negation of being but its deepest fulfillment: the complete alignment of divine *qi* with the world's wounded flow, so that all may be restored to harmony.

3.5 Christological Implications: The Way of Soft Power

When Christology centers on *wu wei* and *kenosis*, the orientation of Christian thought shifts profoundly. Jesus is no longer conceived primarily as a metaphysical exception to human nature or a juridical substitute for human sin. Instead, he emerges as the paradigmatic embodiment of harmonized relational power, the one who walks the Way of Dao to its fullest depth:

- His teaching is not coercive logic but an invitation into the rhythm of grace: "Come to me, all you that are weary . . . . For my yoke is easy, and my burden is light" (Matt 11:28–30).
- His miracles are not spectacular interruptions of natural law but restorations of natural harmony—disabled people walking, the blind seeing, the storm calmed, each a reattunement of disordered *qi* to its original flow.
- His death is not cosmic punishment but the yielding of divine *Sin-ki* into the wound of the world, so that life may spring again.
- His resurrection is not a military conquest of death but the reverberation of love through the fractured field of history.

Such Christology calls us to reimagine divine power. No longer is God the almighty architect who engineers history from above, nor the sovereign judge who rules through decree. In Christodao, divine power flows in compassion, self-emptying rhythm, and yielding strength. It resonates with Zhang Zai's (1022–77) cosmological confession: "Heaven is my father and Earth is my mother, and I, a small being, dwell between them."[2] Christ is that relational dwelling—embodied, humble, attuned—holding heaven and earth in the embrace of reconciled *qi*.

To follow such a Christ is not to master a set of doctrines, nor to wage a campaign for ideological victory. It is to tune one's life to his resonance—to walk in *orthodao*, to embody the same gentle strength that bends without breaking, yields without vanishing,

2. Zhang, "Western Inscription," 690.

and restores without overpowering. In this, discipleship becomes not the defense of theological propositions but the cultivation of an attuned presence in a dissonant world.

3.6 Toward Orthodao: From Belief to Embodied Walking

In the Christodao paradigm, discipleship is neither *orthodoxy* (right belief) nor *orthopraxis* (right action) alone. It is *orthodao*: walking the Way rightly, in relational resonance with Christ, the Dao, and the living flow of *qi*. *Orthodao* is not mystical withdrawal from the world, nor is it the restless activism that exhausts itself in striving. It is the middle path of embodied wisdom—compassionate yet discerning, yielding yet resilient, attuned yet grounded. It is an ethics of presence, cultivated through ongoing practice rather than instant mastery.

To walk *orthodao* is:

- to yield without collapsing;
- to speak without overpowering;
- to act without striving;
- to teach without clinging;
- to suffer without bitterness;
- to love without possession.

In this way, *orthodao* embodies the rhythm of *wu wei* and *kenosis*, transposed into the register of everyday life. It resists the modern world's addiction to acceleration, control, and force, inviting instead the slow, deep rhythm of the Christ who "emptied himself" (Phil 2:7), not to vanish but to become the living pulse of the world. Here, Christian faith becomes a pilgrimage rather than a fortress, a journey rather than a verdict. The church, walking *orthodao*, becomes less an institution of control and more a community of resonance—open to the Spirit's flow, attuned to the cries of creation, yielding to the rhythms of grace.

This is the posture that prepares the disciple for the next Christodao movement: Jesus as *Seonbi*, the Confucian scholar-sage, who embodies moral cultivation, cultural refinement, and the fearless pursuit of justice without coercion. Before we walk that path, we pause here to remember: The Christ we follow is always moving—walking, yielding, flowing—not merely the Truth but the Path that walks.

CHAPTER 4

The New *Taiji*: Jesus and the Harmony of Opposites

Cross, Reversal, and the Paradox of Strength in Weakness

4.1 Introduction: *Taiji* and the Harmony of Opposites

In classical East Asian cosmology, the *Taiji*—literally, the "Great Ultimate"—represents the generative tension and unity of *yin* and *yang*, the fundamental dualities that animate all of existence. *Taiji* is not a fixed object or divine being but a cosmic process: the dynamic source from which the myriad things arise through rhythm, reversal, and resonance. The *yin–yang* diagram, widely recognized yet often misunderstood, is not a picture of dualism but a *cosmology of transformation that becomes a theology of resonance*: Within every fullness, emptiness is hidden; within every rising, a return is implied. In Christodao, this rhythm is received as a vision of salvation through harmony, reversal, and renewal.

In this chapter, we read Jesus through the lens of *Taiji*, interpreting his paradoxical identity—divine and human, powerful and humble, exalted through suffering—as a Daoic harmonization of opposites. From incarnation to cross, Jesus does not resolve tensions by erasing them; he inhabits them, embodying the rhythm of *yin* and *yang* in the Christodao key. In doing so, we come to see that Jesus is not simply a moral exemplar or metaphysical synthesis but what we might call the *New Taiji*: the crucified and risen one in whom cosmic balance is restored, not by force but through self-emptying resonance and reversal.

4.2 *Yin–Yang* and the Cruciform Paradox

According to the *Book of Changes* (*Yi Jing* / *I Ching*) and early Daoian–Confucian cosmology, the interplay of *yin* and *yang* explains all becoming: night and day, softness and hardness, stillness and motion, receptivity and action.[1] Importantly, *yin* and *yang* are not static substances or moral opposites; they are mutually arising, perpetually transforming, and always interdependent.[2] In this frame, *yin* is not weakness but creative potential; *yang* is not dominance but expressive unfolding. Cosmic harmony lies not in the triumph of one over the other but in their mutual rhythm, an oscillating dance that mirrors the pulse of *qi* throughout the universe.

This *yin–yang* logic finds profound Christological resonance in the paradox of the cross. The apostle Paul declares that Christ "emptied himself . . . becoming obedient to the point of death—even death on a cross" (Phil 2:6–8), and that "the weakness of God is stronger than human strength" (1 Cor 1:25). In these passages, we hear the Daoic wisdom of reversal: power hidden in weakness, glory veiled in shame, fullness found in emptiness. Just as *Taiji* gives rise to life through tension and flow, the crucified Christ becomes the cosmic axis where divine reversal is made flesh. His surrender is not defeat but the deeper movement of the Way—*wu wei* in cruciform rhythm. He does not annihilate opposites; he reconciles them in his own body, stretched between heaven and earth.

1. Wilhelm, *Book of Changes*, xllx–lvii.
2. Chan, *Source Book*, 263–66.

4.3 Glory in Weakness: The Dao of Reversal

The *Dao De Jing* speaks often in paradox: "The soft and weak overcome the hard and strong" (36). "He who humbles himself will be raised" (66). In the Christodao reading, this paradox—the low becoming exalted, the soft overcoming the hard—is not accidental but fundamental to understanding the life, death, and resurrection of Jesus. Jesus does not ascend by triumph but descends in love. His authority is not imposed but received; his reign comes not through conquest but through yielding, forgiving, and dying. He rides a donkey, not a war horse (Matt 21:5); he allows a woman to anoint him with costly oil (Mark 14:3–9); he submits to arrest, mockery, and crucifixion without resistance.

Yet it is through this *yin*-movement that the deepest *yang* of resurrection emerges. The cross, far from being a theological problem to be explained away, becomes the ultimate symbol of cosmic inversion and Daoic alignment. In this movement, Jesus becomes the *New Taiji*—the one in whom the wounded center holds, where all polarities are reconciled not by negation but by transformative flow. The Christian tradition has long wrestled with paradox—Jesus as true God and true human, suffering servant and risen Lord—but Christodao offers a cosmological grammar that treats paradox not as a problem to solve but as a rhythm to follow. The cross is not an exception to Dao but its most complete expression.

4.4 The Cross as Cosmic Inversion

In Daoic cosmology, the *movement of reversal* (*fan*) is not a deviation from order but the Way's most natural rhythm. The *Dao De Jing* affirms: "Reversal is the movement of Dao" (40). This principle helps us see the crucifixion of Jesus not as an interruption of cosmic order but as its most mysterious and profound alignment. In Christodao, the cross is not an anomaly but a *cosmic Taiji moment*: The *yin* of surrender yields the *yang* of renewal; the shame of death conceives the glory of resurrection.

Traditional theology often views the cross through juridical or sacrificial lenses. But Christodao reimagines the cross as *cosmic inversion*, in which *the weakness of God is stronger than human strength* (1 Cor 1:25), and life springs forth from yielding. This is not merely symbolic. The crucified Christ becomes the *pivot of Taiji*, the harmonizing center where all dualities—life and death, divine and human, exaltation and abasement—interpenetrate.

In Daoic terms, the cross is where softness overcomes hardness, not through violence but by *wu wei*—non-coercive love that shapes reality from within. The crucified Christ is the living axis of reversal, the cosmic hinge upon which the world's healing turns.[3]

4.5 Jesus as the New *Taiji*

Taiji is not simply a theory of balance; it is the generative rhythm of the cosmos, the dynamic unity from which *yin* and *yang* produce the "ten thousand things." In Confucian cosmology, particularly in the works of Zhou Dunyi (1017–73) and Zhu Xi (1130–1200), *Taiji* is the origin of harmony, the dynamic One that differentiates yet unites all things.[4]

To call Jesus the New *Taiji* is to acknowledge that he is not only the reconciler of God and humanity but also the harmonizing pulse of the universe itself. In him, paradox is not erased but held; glory is veiled in weakness, death becomes the seed of life, and the fragmentation of creation begins to knit together. As Zhang Zai's *Western Inscription* proclaims, "Heaven is my father and Earth is my mother, and even such a small creature as I find an intimate place in their midst."

In this frame, Christ is the relational embodiment of that cosmic intimacy—the one who not only teaches harmony but *embodies the harmony of heaven and earth*. The cross becomes the cruciform *Taiji*, the site of divine reversal in which *yin* and *yang* spiral into new creation. Jesus is thus not a static synthesis

3. For a proto expression of Christodao by Ryu Young-mo (1890–1981), see H. Kim, *Theology of Dao*, 147–68.

4. See Adler, *Reconstructing the Confucian Dao*, 45–52.

of natures but a living field of transformation, the one whose Dao enfolds the universe into reconciliation.

4.6 Christodao Implications: Harmony, Ethics, and Discipleship

Seeing Jesus as the New *Taiji* carries profound implications for Christian ethics, spirituality, and ecclesial identity. If Christ embodies cosmic inversion and the rhythm of *yin–yang*, then discipleship is not about enforcing dualisms but learning to walk in harmony—to live in *orthodao*, "right balance."

This balance is not a mere compromise; it is a spiritual discipline of:

- yielding without servility;
- acting without aggression;
- speaking without domination;
- leading without control;
- dying into life.

In a world torn by binaries—strong/weak, right/left, sacred/secular—the Christodao vision offers a path beyond antagonism: the Way of paradox held in peace. This is not relativism but reconciling rhythm, born from the crucified Dao.

Churches shaped by this vision become communities of resonance, not control. Spiritual formation becomes the cultivation of *a Taiji-like poise,* characterized by presence, compassion, and kenotic wisdom. Such communities embody the cross not as an ideology but as an energetic center—holding grief and joy, sorrow and praise in sacred tension. In this, Jesus—crucified and risen—is the *New Taiji*: not merely the teacher of wisdom but its living field, its wounded harmony, its cosmic reconciliation. To follow him is to live in rhythm with reversal, to become both still and flowing, soft and resilient, human and divine.

Jesus as the New Taiji

Reversal–*orthodao*
(right balance)

Figure 1: Jesus as the New *Taiji*

CHAPTER 5

Jesus as *Seonbi*: The Sage of Virtue and Compassion

Confucian Moral Cultivation and Christological Virtue

5.1 Introduction: Jesus as *Seonbi*

IN THE EVOLVING VISION of Christodao, we have considered Jesus as Dao, as *Qi*, as *Hodos*, and as the New *Taiji*—the crucified center of paradox and transformation. Here, we turn to another Confucian tradition, and particularly to the Korean cultural idiom of the *Seonbi*, to deepen our grasp of the ethical embodiment of Christ's Way.

The *Seonbi*, historically situated within the Neo-Confucian ethos of the Joseon dynasty (1392–1910), was more than an academic scholar. A *Seonbi* embodied the Dao through rigorous moral cultivation, integrity in public life, and a commitment to compassionate teaching or governance—even outside positions of institutional authority. Known for poverty, humility, quiet wisdom, and unwavering moral clarity, *Seonbi* figures resisted political corruption and social injustice at personal cost.

To envision Jesus as *Seonbi* is not to domesticate his radical message into Confucian propriety but to recognize that his life reflects Confucian virtue ethics lived in the flesh. He not only proclaimed truth but walked the Way of righteousness (*yi*), compassion (*ren*), and self-cultivation (*xiu shen*). He taught by embodiment, resisted domination without violence, and called his followers not to revere him from a distance but to follow him in a life of moral resonance.

5.2 The Ethical Grammar of *Seonbi* Culture

In Korean Neo-Confucianism, the *Seonbi* ideal centered on three interwoven virtues:

- *Moral integrity*: uprightness and uncompromising ethical stance.
- *Compassionate empathy*: the compassionate heart, sensitive to the suffering of others.
- *Self-cultivation*: continual learning and refinement of character.

These were not abstract ideals but the fruit of disciplined reflection, emotional refinement, and concrete practice in daily life. The *Seonbi* aligned themselves with heaven's principle (*Tianli*) not by withdrawing from society but by walking within it with moral clarity and humility. Toegye Yi Hwang (1501–70)—a Korean *Seonbi* prototype—wrote that to study is to cultivate the mind-heart so that it may become reverent and clear.[1] Without cultivation, one cannot embody the principle of heaven in one's life. The *Seonbi* was thus not a philosopher detached from action but a living vessel of Dao—harmonizing heaven, self, and community through moral resonance.

This posture was inherently kenotic: humility above status, quiet above spectacle, resilience above reaction. Such qualities resonate with the Christodao pattern—Jesus as one who yields without weakness, heals without control, and teaches without domination, through moral transparency and compassion.

1. See Yi, *To Become a Sage*, 21–23, 117–25.

5.3 Jesus and the Path of Embodied Virtue

The Gospels portray Jesus not only as a divine figure but as one who *embodies virtue in relational action.* His life can be re-read through the ethical grammar of *Seonbi* culture:

- *Moral integrity*: Jesus speaks truth to power, not for provocation but for integrity's sake. He calls out hypocrisy (Matt 23), resists worldly honors (Luke 14:7–11), and remains faithful even in the face of death.
- *Compassionate empathy*: Jesus feels deeply for those suffering. He weeps at Lazarus's tomb (John 11:35), heals the blind and the marginalized (Mark 10:46–52), and speaks tenderly to the outcast woman (Luke 7:36–50). His compassion is not sentimental; it flows from deep moral resonance with others' pain.
- *Self-cultivation*: Jesus retreats to pray (Mark 1:35), studies and teaches Scripture (Luke 4:16–21), and invites his disciples into *lifelong formation*: "Take my yoke upon you and learn from me" (Matt 11:29).

Like a *Seonbi,* Jesus rejects social advancement for moral clarity. Like *Seonbi,* he lives in the margins but exerts a gravitational ethical pull. And like *Seonbi,* his words are inseparable from his way of life. His authority does not astonish us because it is loud but because it is deeply integrated (Matt 7:28–29).

In the Christodao vision, Jesus as *Seonbi* is not a cultural borrowing but a *contextual unveiling*—a way of seeing how the Way becomes flesh in a Korean ethical idiom, without losing its universality. It is Jesus, fully divine and fully human, walking the *virtue-shaped Dao of heaven.* This perspective is a theme explored more deeply in my first published book, *Wang Yang-ming and Karl Barth: A Confucian-Christian Dialogue* (1996).

5.4 The Beatitudes and Confucian Virtue Cultivation

Among the teachings of Jesus, none better reflect the *Seonbi* spirit than the Beatitudes (Matt 5:1–12). Spoken not to rulers or religious elites but to ordinary people on a mountainside, these blessings invert conventional values: "Blessed are the poor in spirit . . . the meek . . . the merciful . . . the pure in heart . . . the peacemakers . . . those who are persecuted for righteousness' sake." Each of these virtues—humility, mercy, purity, peacemaking, moral endurance—finds striking resonance in the Confucian tradition of *virtue cultivation*.

Confucius taught that moral development begins in the family and community but is rooted in personal refinement: "To cultivate oneself and thereby bring peace to the people is the highest virtue."[2] This process begins with *the mind and heart* (*xin*), where Four Beginnings (*sidan*)—compassion (*ren*), righteousness (*yi*), propriety (*li*), and wisdom (*zhi*)—are nurtured into full maturity through practice and reflection.[3] The Beatitudes, too, reflect a gradual unfolding of the *Dao of inner transformation*: not imposed commandments but a spiritual map of ethical becoming.

Jesus, like a sage, speaks from the mountain—not to declare law but to *offer a vision of flourishing* that is relational, humble, and morally courageous. The poor in spirit become rich in moral clarity; the persecuted become blessed in solidarity. His ethical vision aligns with Toegye's ideal of *cultivating sincerity* (*cheng*), which aims to harmonize inner sincerity with the flourishing of the entire community, ultimately transforming one's entire being and community.[4]

5.5 Toward a Virtue-Centered Christology

In traditional Western Christology, the focus often falls on *ontological categories* (divine vs. human) or *soteriological mechanics*

2. Confucius, *Analects*, 14.42.
3. See Mencius, *Works of Mencius*, Book 2A.
4. See Chung, *Korean Neo-Confucianism*, 92–95.

(atonement, substitution). But in the Christodao vision—especially through the lens of *Seonbi* Jesus—Christology becomes *ethical and formative*: not only who Christ is but how Christ becomes the Way we walk. Jesus is not simply the teacher of virtue; he is *virtue-in-relation*:

- His *compassion* (*ren*) is not abstract but enacted in his healing and embrace of the socially excluded.
- His *righteousness* (*yi*) is seen in his fearless confrontation with injustice (e.g., cleansing the temple; Matt 21:12–13).
- His *ritual integrity* (*li*) is observed in his faithfulness to communal practices, such as Sabbath prayer, while also transcending them with ethical wisdom.
- His *moral discernment* (*zhi*) shines in his parables and his silence before Pilate (John 18:38).

This kind of Christology aligns with *Dao-centered cultivation*, where salvation is not juridical pardon but *the transformation of the heart-mind* (*xing*). In the Christodao idiom, Jesus is not just Savior but a *model of virtue embodied in context*, the living *Seonbi* whose Way harmonizes heaven and earth through relational compassion.

5.6 Orthodao Formation and Moral Resonance

To follow *Seonbi* Jesus is not to memorize rules or profess beliefs but to *walk the Way of character* to cultivate *orthodao* through relational wisdom. This involves slow and rhythmic formation:

- *silence and self-examination* rather than self-assertion;
- *compassion* over competition;
- *steady learning* as an act of devotion;
- *civic engagement without egoic ambition;*
- *integrity* over expediency.

The church, in this view, becomes not a fortress of doctrine but a *community of formation*, where disciples follow Christ the *Seonbi* through lived resonance. The goal is not perfection but *sincerity* (*cheng*): *to become persons who harmonize heaven's Way with everyday virtue*. This approach also opens space for interreligious humility.

Confucian sages and Christian saints may walk in parallel rhythms. Christodao does not erase doctrinal differences but honors them within a *shared ethical resonance*. In the language of the *doctrine of the mean* (*Zhongyong*), "Sincerity is the Way of heaven. To reflect upon it is the Way of humanity" (ch. 20).

Thus, Christ the *Seonbi* is not a moralistic overlay but the *living Way of virtue that flows from Dao, enters into flesh, and returns again through practice*. In him, heaven's principle and human life embrace—softly, steadily, and with unwavering moral clarity.

CHAPTER 6

Christ and the Relational Universe

Interbeing, Ganying, and the Relational Body of Christ

6.1 Introduction: A Daoic Universe of Relation

In the Christodao vision, theology begins not with an isolated being but with *relational becoming*. As we have seen in earlier chapters, Jesus is not a static essence but a walking Way (*hodos*), a harmonizing field (*Taiji*), and a compassionate sage (*Seonbi*). In this chapter, we explore how Christ, as Dao, resonates within a *relational universe*—one shaped by *interdependence, mutual arising, and cosmic resonance.*

Daoic cosmology affirms that *nothing exists in isolation.* All things arise together, change together, and return together. *Zhuangzi* proclaims: "Heaven and Earth were born with me, and the ten thousand things are one with me."[1] This is not metaphor but cosmology: The cosmos is a *web of relations*, a field of subtle flows, *a choreography of resonance*. Similarly, in the Gospel of John, Christ is not merely alongside creation but "in the beginning" with it—and "all things came into being through him" (John 1:3). *This cosmic Christ is not external to the world but its connective rhythm.*

The question is not whether Christ relates to the world but *how* he resonates within it. Daoic thought and East Asian

1. Zhuangzi, *Complete Works*, ch. 2.

Pneumatology offer a grammar—*qi*, *ganying*, and *Sin-ki*—by which we can speak of Christ as a *relational mediator in a universe of resonance.*

6.2 Interbeing and Mutual Arising

The Vietnamese Zen master Thich Nhat Hanh (1926–2022) coined the term *"interbeing"* to describe the Buddhist vision of co-arising reality: "You cannot be by yourself alone. You must inter-be with every other thing."[2] This vision is paralleled in the Daoic principle of mutual arising, which posits that all opposites, events, and lives come into being not through separation but through *relational polarity and cyclical emergence.* As *Dao De Jing* (2) says: "Being and non-being give birth to each other. Difficult and easy complete each other. Long and short define each other."

In this cosmology, reality is never fixed but always *arises in mutual interaction.* A tree exists not apart from the soil, sun, or sky; it breathes them into form. Human identity, likewise, emerges only in *relation to others, history, and heaven.* This vision resonates with a *panentheistic Christology*, in which Christ is neither separated from creation nor dissolved into it but *dwells in all things while transcending them.*[3] Paul writes, "In him all things hold together" (Col 1:17). This holding is not mechanical but *relational*—Christ as *qi-like resonance*, sustaining and animating the cosmic field.

6.3 Christ as Mediator of Relational Resonance

In classical theology, Christ is often referred to as the *mediator* between God and humanity. Yet in Christodao, this mediation is not a bridge over a metaphysical gap but a *harmonizing presence within the Daoic flow*. The Dao does not dominate or divide; it flows. Likewise, Christ mediates not by standing apart but by *participating deeply in the rhythms of all things*. This relational

2. Hanh, *Interbeing*, 3–4.

3. See Keller, *Cloud of the Impossible*, 21, 33.

mediation may be named through the Daoic concept of *ganying*, often translated as "resonant responsiveness." *Ganying* describes how *resonance connects heaven, earth, and humanity*—how the cry of one thing calls forth a subtle, responsive echo in another.[4] Jesus' life is full of such *ganying*:

- His compassion evokes faith in the suffering (Mark 5:34).
- His silence moves Pilate to bewilderment (John 18:38).
- His breath brings peace to a fearful room (John 20:22).

These are not magical acts but moments of *subtle resonance*—*Sin-ki* flowing outward, received and returned. Christ as mediator does not force transformation; he *draws it forth through presence*, through the *Daoic field of response*. Thus, mediation becomes not a doctrine but a practice of *attuned relationality*. Christ is the one in whom the cosmos feels itself, heals itself, and flows again in tune with Dao.

6.4 Beyond Dualism: Resonance as Ontology

Western theology has long operated within *metaphysical dualisms*, such as spirit and matter, Creator and creation, and divine and human. Even in efforts to overcome these binaries, Christology has often re-inscribed them—Jesus as the bridge over the gap, the mediator between two incompatible natures. In the Christodao vision, however, dualism gives way to *resonance*. Daoic cosmology does not divide being but perceives reality as *woven through dynamic relations*. Existence is not a set of substances but a field of responsive flows—*ganying*—in which beings influence and are influenced, echoing across time and space.

To exist is to *resonate*, to move in response to the Dao. In this context, *ontology is no longer a fixed essence but a relational vibration*. This is not relativism or formless mysticism but a rigorous alternative cosmology: one where coherence is found not in immutability but in *co-arising rhythm*. From this angle, Christ

4. See Ziporyn, *Ironies of Oneness and Difference*, 95–100.

does not resolve dualisms through synthesis but *transcends them through resonance*. He embodies not "spirit" against "body," but *qi*-infused flesh. He reveals not transcendence as detachment but as *deep relational presence*.

In this way, Christ is not merely the God-human. He is the *fullness of relational existence*, the one in whom we feel the Dao pulsing most clearly, who holds all things together, not through force but through *resonant responsiveness* (Col 1:17).

6.5 Incarnation as *Ganying*: The Relational Body of Christ

If resonance is the structure of the cosmos, then the incarnation is its *intensification*. In the Gospel of John, the Logos becomes flesh (1:14), not as a metaphysical contradiction but as *a relational event*—Dao entering the web of mutual arising. This can be understood through the concept of *ganying*, which describes *sympathetic responsiveness across distance*. One life resonates with another across time and space through unseen but real energetic threads.

The incarnation of Jesus becomes the *cosmic ganying of divine compassion*: heaven responding to earth, earth responding to heaven, and all things realigned in the flow. His life is a field of resonance:

- He weeps, and others awaken.
- He breathes, and the Spirit moves.
- He is touched, and healing flows (Mark 5:30).

As my earlier writings note, *Sin-ki*—the spiritual energy of the oppressed—unites with the *primordial qi/ki* of Dao in moments of awakening, such as the *Ugeumchi* phenomenon.[5] In Jesus, this relational alignment becomes fully visible. His body is not just a sacrificial object but a *living instrument of ganying*, in which divine vitality moves outward to awaken, heal, and restore. The incarnation is thus not a singular event but an *ongoing rhythm*. Christ's presence continues in the cosmos through every act of

5. See H. Kim, *Theology of Dao*, 46–53.

compassion, every breath of Spirit, every moment of harmony that ripples into the collective *Sin-ki* of creation.

6.6 Orthodao and Resonant Discipleship

The theological implications of Christ in a relational universe call us again to *orthodao*: not mere right belief (*orthodoxy*) or right action (*orthopraxis*) but *right resonance* with the Way. Orthodao is the practice of *harmonizing one's life with Christ's resonance*, not by imitation alone but *by participation in the cosmic rhythm he embodies*. This invites a new kind of discipleship—one that is:

- *relational* rather than hierarchical;
- *attuned* rather than assertive;
- *ecological* rather than anthropocentric;
- *contemplative and connective*, grounded in sensing, listening, and responding.

To walk the *orthodao* path is to become a living *ganying* point, mediating between heaven and earth through presence, compassion, and alignment. It means to breathe with the breath of Christ, to heal with the gentleness of *wu wei*, and to speak only from the resonance of love. In the Daoic-Christian convergence, this is not vague mysticism; it is *embodied Pneumatology*. As in *Process Theology*, God is not the coercive architect of outcomes but "the lure toward relational intensity."[6] Christ is the concrete form of that lure: *The pulse of Dao becomes flesh*.

In the Christodao vision, then, the cosmos is not a machine but a resonance field. Christ is not an exception to it but its *center and song*. To follow him is to attune one's heart to the soundless music of the Way and to live as one who "inter-is" with all things.

6. See Cobb and Griffin, *Process Theology*, 43–47.

CHAPTER 7

Soteriology as Harmonization

Fan, Wu Wei, and the Renewal of Resonance

7.1 Introduction: Salvation as Cosmic Resonance

TRADITIONAL CHRISTIAN SOTERIOLOGY HAS often been framed in *legal or metaphysical terms*: sin as guilt, salvation as pardon, and Christ as a substitute who satisfies divine justice. While this juridical model served Western theological frameworks, it struggles to speak compellingly to East Asian sensibilities, which are shaped by *relational cosmology, moral cultivation*, and the rhythm of *harmonic balance.*

In the Christodao vision, salvation is not a transaction between God and the individual but the *restoration of relational resonance* between heaven, earth, humanity, and all creation. Salvation is not escape from the world but *realignment with the flow of Dao*, the deep harmonies of life, breath, and being. To be saved is to be *healed of dissonance*—to return to the Way, to participate in the *sociocosmic renewal* of what has been fragmented. Jesus, as Christodao, does not rescue us from the world but *reweaves us into its deepest rhythm* through non-coercive love, kenotic resonance, and restorative presence.

7.2 Sin as Disharmony, Not Guilt

In Daoian and Confucian thought, wrongdoing is not primarily a matter of law or jurisprudence but a rupture in the relational flow—a failure to live in accord with the Dao, to cultivate virtue, or to sustain the harmony of the community and cosmos. Sin, in this view, is *disharmony*, and its consequences are not punishment but imbalance, stagnation, and alienation.

This vision resonates deeply with biblical images of *shalom*—a Hebrew term often translated as "peace," but more accurately meaning *wholeness, flourishing, and justice in right relationship*. As Walter Brueggemann notes, "Shalom is the central vision of the Hebrew Bible's hope for a reconciled creation."[1]

In Christodao, *sin is the breakdown of resonance*:

- between the self and the Dao;
- between human communities;
- between humanity and earth;
- between heaven and the created world.

This echoes the *Dao De Jing*'s warning that "when Dao is lost, virtue appears; when virtue is lost, morality appears; when morality is lost, rules arise" (38). The deeper the disharmony, the more society turns to coercive systems to regulate what has already unraveled. Thus, Christ does not save by satisfying wrath but by *restoring resonance*. He returns us not to innocence but to *harmony*—with each other, with the cosmos, and with the divine rhythm of the Way.

7.3 Salvation as Return (*Fan*): A Daoic Realignment

In the Daoic worldview, all things arise and return in rhythm. The *Dao De Jing* declares, "Reversal is the movement of Dao" (40). Return (*fan*) is not regression but *renewal*—the turning back from deviation to realignment with the creative source. To be saved,

1. Brueggemann, *Peace*, 13–17.

then, is to be *brought back into tune*, like a dissonant string returning to pitch.

This aligns powerfully with the biblical vision of *metanoia*—often translated as repentance, but more accurately rendered as *"turning" or "returning"* (e.g., Luke 15:20). The parable of the prodigal son is not about moral condemnation but about the *movement of return and reconciliation*—to the father, to the household, to joy. In Amos, salvation is not escape from judgment but the *restoration of justice*: "Let justice roll down like waters, and righteousness like an ever-flowing stream" (5:24).

In the Christodao frame, salvation is the *reconvergence of all dissonant forces—qi, Sin-ki*, ecological imbalance, systemic injustice—into a flow of healing. Christ, as Dao made flesh, becomes the one who enacts this return not by coercion but by *yielding into the stream and reversing the flood.*

This return is especially visible in the *Ugeumchi* phenomenon, in which feeble fish swim upstream not by power but by resonance. Salvation here is not escape from the stream but a *creative leap toward the origin*, guided by *the upward current hidden within the downward force*. This is Christ as cosmic return: the harmonizer of lost rhythms, the one who brings the Way back to itself through embodied love.

7.4 Grace as Relational Restoration: *Wu Wei* and Divine Resonance

In classical Western theology, *grace* is often understood as a *divine gift of unmerited favor*—a one-sided act of divine initiative to override human incapacity. Yet in the *Christodao* paradigm, grace appears not as an interruption of the world's order but as *a restoration of its deepest relational rhythm*. Grace is Dao in motion: the return of harmony, the healing of fragmentation, the *reopening of resonance* between heaven and earth.

This is well captured by the Daoic concept of *wu wei*, which we encountered in chapter 3. *Wu wei* does not mean inaction but *non-coercive action*—doing without forcing, responding without domination, aligning with the flow rather than striving against it. In the same way, *grace is not divine imposition but divine resonance*—Dao flowing into the dissonance of sin, *not to crush it but to tune it back into the harmony of the whole.*

Jesus' entire ministry unfolds in *wu wei*:

- He acts not from strategic control but *deep attunement.*
- He offers healing not through spectacle but *compassionate presence.*
- He yields in death not as defeat but as *the deepest pulse of grace flowing into the fracture of creation.*

Thus, grace in Christodao is not merely pardon; it is *relational restoration.* It is *God's Daoic resonance with our Sin-ki*, not cancelling it but converting it into returning energy. It is not supernatural intrusion but *the most natural harmony reawakened.*

7.5 The *Ugeumchi* Christ: Salvation Through Collective *Sin-Ki*

This vision is vividly expressed in the *Ugeumchi* phenomenon, as developed in my earlier writings.[2] The image of fish ascending against the horrifying downward current of the flood, through the union of their *Sin-ki* with the countervailing upward flow, becomes a *Christological parable of salvific resistance.* This story is not simply a metaphor but a *soteriological grammar* grounded in East Asian anthropology and Pneumatology. The oppressed do not rise through violence but through aligning their collective energy with the primordial current of Dao—a reversal achieved *through resonance.*

Jesus, in this vision, becomes the archetypal *Ugeumchi* fish—*the one who aligns his Sin-ki with the hidden flow of God in the midst of history's demonic currents.* His crucifixion is not a failure but a *Daoic reversal*: the *yin* of surrender giving birth to the *yang* of resurrection. His rise is not a private miracle but *the reawakening*

2. See H. Kim, *Christ and the Tao*, 138–48; H. Kim, *Theology of Dao*, 18–33.

of cosmic Sin-ki, empowering the *minjung*, the wounded earth, and the abandoned peoples to rise. Salvation here is not individualistic ascent but *the collective reversal of broken history* through harmonization with Christ's path. It is the *sociocosmic redemption* of the marginalized, not by escaping suffering but by flowing *through it into generative return.*

7.6 Orthodao and the Harmonizing Life: From Redemption to Resonance

What then is salvation lived? It is not merely to believe one has been saved, nor to behave according to religious law. In Christodao, *salvation becomes orthodao: to walk in harmony with Christ's restorative resonance*. This orthodao is both inward and outward. It involves:

- the *cultivation of attunement*;
- the *practice of compassionate resonance*;
- the *ethical reorientation of systems* toward balance and mutual flourishing.

Orthodao is not passive harmony but *engaged restoration*—to act with *wu wei* against structural coercion, to speak with resonance into alienation, to return with *fan* toward justice and shalom. It is to participate in what Amos envisioned: the *restoration of life as* flowing with justice, where "righteousness like an everflowing stream" (Amos 5:24) becomes not just a metaphor but an ecological, communal, and spiritual rhythm.

In this rhythm, the church is called to be *a community of harmonizers*—not judges of salvation but witnesses to Dao. Their life together should pulse with *restored resonance*, echoing Christ's own *Sin-ki* as a healing wave within the relational universe. Ultimately, salvation in Christodao is not merely about where we go when we die but also *how we return* now to the source of life, *how we walk the Way of balance* in a fragmented world, and *how we rise*—not alone but *with all creation*—into restored resonance.

CHAPTER 8

The Dao of the Resurrection

Resurrection as Rhythmic Renewal and Ecological Hope

8.1 Introduction: Resurrection as Rhythmic Renewal

AMONG ALL CHRISTIAN DOCTRINES, the resurrection of Jesus has most often been framed in terms of a supernatural triumph: a breaking of the natural order, a divine interruption of death, and a proof of victory. Yet such interpretations—especially in Western theology—risk severing the resurrection from its deeper, cosmic, *and relational meaning*.

In the Christodao vision, resurrection is not an exception to Dao but its *deepest rhythm*: the return of life through the cycles of death and decay, the unfolding of *unceasing vitality*, the ceaseless generation of the ten thousand things. Jesus does not transcend nature in resurrection; he embodies its most profound movement. The resurrection is thus not an anomaly but *harmony restored*. Christ rises not against Dao but *with* it, enacting the *movement of fan*—the return. His body is not a magical object but the crystallization of Daoic life energy, realigned, reawakened, and released.

In this chapter, we will explore how the resurrection of Christ serves as a pattern of renewal for all creation—cosmic, communal, and ethical. It invites believers not merely to believe in life after death but to live now in the pulse of the *regenerative Dao.*

8.2 The Cycle of Death and Life: Dao and the Deep Ecology of Resurrection

Daoic cosmology teaches that death is not the opposite of life but *its transformation*. The *Dao De Jing* affirms: "All things are born of being. Being is born of non-being" (40). And "To live is to die, and to die is to return" (16). This cycle is embedded in nature: The leaf falls, decays, nourishes soil, and gives rise to the next generation. In the Confucian-Daoian worldview, *nothing is lost*: All returns not to a static origin but to the *rhythmic source.*

This wisdom resonates with the Gospel vision of death and life in balance: "Unless a grain of wheat falls into the earth and dies, it remains alone; but if it dies, it bears much fruit" (John 12:24). Jesus' own interpretation of his impending death is not as a sacrifice to appease wrath but as a *seed in the soil of Dao*, waiting to blossom anew. In this cosmology, resurrection is not a supernatural intrusion but a *natural culmination*. It is the *soft power of life reasserting itself*, the realignment of *qi*, the return of vitality into a wounded field. Jesus' resurrection becomes the *pulse of ecological renewal*, a vision of creation not condemned but restored.

8.3 *Fan*: Resurrection as Cosmic Return

In the *Dao De Jing* (40), we read: "Reversal (*fan*) is the movement of Dao. Weakness is the use of Dao." This is the theological heart of Christodao resurrection: reversal not as rupture but as return. *Fan* is not a detour but the Way itself—*death folding into life, despair reversing into hope, defeat transfiguring into new creation.*

Jesus' resurrection enacts this *fan* not only personally but cosmically. The resurrection of Christ:

- *returns the human story* from empire to communion;
- *returns history* from crucifixion to reconciliation;
- *returns creation* from exploitation to breath and blessing.

In this way, resurrection is not merely about the immortality of an individual *but about the reawakening of the relational field.* It is the *Sin-ki* of *Ugeumchi* leaping again, not because death was avoided but because it was *entered fully, then reversed in rhythm.* As Zhuangzi imagines the transformation of death: "Life is the companion of death; death is the beginning of life. Who knows where one ends, and the other begins?"[1]

In Jesus, this threshold is crossed not in fear but in *trustful harmony*. He does not resist death; he walks into it in *wu wei* and *returns in fan.*

8.4 Resurrection as *Sin-Ki* Renewal and Rhythmic Release

In the *Ugeumchi* phenomenon, as Kim Chi-ha vividly recounts, the feeble fish swim against the flood not through muscular might but through the mysterious alignment of their *Sin-ki* with the *yin* upward flow hidden beneath the downward current. This poetic vision provides us with a Christodao grammar for the resurrection: not the conquering *of death by external force but the rising of life through resonant alignment.*

Resurrection, in this view, is not an intrusion of external power but *a releasing of internal vitality—the return of Sin-ki to its cosmic source and task.* Christ rises not alone but as the *first pulse of a renewed collective vitality, a resonant field of renewal* in which the life force of all creation begins again.

This is also reflected in the Hebrew understanding of the Spirit as *ruach*—breath, wind, life-force—moving over the chaos of creation (Gen 1:2) and returning to raise dry bones (Ezek 37). Jesus' resurrection is *not merely the reversal of death* but also the *restoration of Spirit-breath to a fractured cosmos.* It is the *qi rising*

1. Zhuangzi, *Complete Works*, ch. 22.

again, not primarily as individual survival but as the *rhythmic breath of Dao re-inhaled into creation*. In this sense, resurrection is not the end of Jesus' story but the *unfolding of the Way he embodied all along*—soft strength, non-coercive love, resonant compassion, and relational healing. His *Sin-ki* becomes the generative pulse that renews the field of life itself.

8.5 The Ethical Pulse of Resurrection: Ecology, Justice, and Compassion

If resurrection is the rhythm of *cosmic renewal*, then it cannot remain a doctrinal claim—it must become *a way of living*. In the Christodao vision, to believe in resurrection is to *embody its reversal* in daily life: to bring harmony where there is violence, to restore balance where there is exploitation, and to sow peace where there is division.

This has *ecological implications*: Resurrection invites us to join the rhythms of earth, to repair what has been ruptured, to live as harmonizers rather than dominators. "Blessed are the meek," says Jesus, "for they shall inherit the earth" (Matt 5:5). In Daoic cosmology, the soft is powerful because it *respects the flow*; the earth heals when we yield to its pulse.

It has *social implications*: Resurrection calls us to see the marginalized as the *first partners of renewal*, as Jesus appears first to the women (John 20:11–18), the doubters (John 20:24–29), and the ashamed (Luke 24:13–35). *Return* (*fan*) is not restoration of status but *transfiguration of relationship*—a new way of seeing, being, and belonging.

It has *spiritual implications*: Resurrection is the path of *moral reweaving*, of *rejoining the field of Dao* in sincerity (*cheng*) and responsiveness (*ganying*). Christ's resurrection invites us into a discipleship of resurrection, not through triumphalism but through *humble orthodao*—to become resonant with the Way that regenerates all things.

8.6 Orthodao as Living Resurrection: Becoming the Way of Renewal

In the final movement of Christodao soteriology, *resurrection becomes vocation*: not only what God has done but also what we are called to live. Orthodao, in this sense, is to walk the *resurrected rhythm*:

- to practice *soft strength* over coercion;
- to live in *returning cycles*, not linear conquest;
- to join the *pulse of justice*, not as ideology but as a healing flow;
- to embody *ganying*—resonant responsiveness—in all things.

Resurrection is the enfolding of chaos into cosmos, not the erasure of difference but the emergence of new relations. In Christodao terms, resurrection is not escape from the ten thousand things but *their re-weaving into Dao through Christ as rhythm.*

The church, then, becomes *a community of reversal* not clinging to power but leaping with the *Sin-ki* of compassion and justice. The Eucharist becomes a celebration of *rhythmic participation*, the embodiment of *fan* and shalom in practice. The body of Christ becomes not dogma, but an *energetic field*. Ultimately, to follow the risen Christ is to walk the Way of Dao, *ever returning, ever renewing*, until all things breathe again in harmony.

CHAPTER 9

Conclusion: Christodao and the Future of Theology

From Paradigm Shift to Orthodao Living

9.1 Christodao Recapitulated: A Theology of the Walking Way

THIS BOOK HAS UNFOLDED a vision of Jesus Christ not as a static object of belief but as *the living Way*—Dao enfleshed, *Sin-ki* in motion, *Taiji* embodied, and *ganying* activated across creation. Christodao offers a Christology rooted not in metaphysical substance nor political abstraction but in *relational resonance, rhythmic reversal, and compassionate presence.*

This vision is summarized in the key concepts of each chapter:

- Jesus as *Dao* (ch. 1): the Way that flows through all things.
- Jesus in *Qi* (ch. 2): the vital energy of divine resonance.
- Jesus as *Hodos* (ch. 3): the non-coercive walker of *wu wei.*
- Jesus as *Taiji* (ch. 4): harmonizer of paradox and opposites.
- Jesus as *Seonbi* (ch. 5): the sage of moral cultivation.
- Jesus in the *relational cosmos* (ch. 6): mediator of *ganying.*
- Jesus in *resurrection* (ch. 8): *fan* as renewal, not rupture.

Each chapter is a turn in the mandala of Christodao: a theology that walks in step with East Asian wisdom, yet speaks to the universal longing for harmony, justice, and sacred presence in the Anthropocene.

9.2 From *Logos* and *Praxis* to Dao: Paradigm Shift and Continuity

Western theology has long oscillated between two macro-paradigms:

- *The logos paradigm*: theology as rational discourse, metaphysical clarity, doctrinal articulation.
- *The praxis paradigm*: theology as historical liberation, social action, and moral protest.

Theodao proposes a *third horizon: the Dao paradigm*—a way of thinking, walking, and becoming that transcends static substance and binary oppositions. The Dao paradigm does not reject logos or praxis but *resituates them within a living field of resonance.* It draws from the deep structures of *East Asian cosmology*, where the world is not a battleground of absolutes but a field of flows: *yin–yang*, *qi*, *wu wei*, and *ganying*.

In this vision:

- theology becomes *attunement*;
- Christology becomes *resonant embodiment*;
- salvation becomes *harmonization*;
- discipleship becomes *orthodao*: walking the Way in sincerity (*cheng*) and wisdom (*zhi*).

9.3 Theological Implications: Cosmos, Ethics, and the Church

The Christodao paradigm has broad implications for Christian theology and community life:

- *Cosmological*: Christ is not an intrusion into creation but its *pulse*, its center of coherence (Col 1:17), its cruciform Dao of return. He heals not by standing apart from the world but by *flowing through its fracture.*
- *Soteriological*: Salvation is not transactional atonement but *collective harmonization*. Jesus does not rescue us from history but calls us to *reverse its violence through Sin-ki alignment.*
- *Ecclesial*: The church becomes not a fortress, program, or institution but a *community of resonance*—practicing *ganying*, restoring *qi*, and living Eucharist as vibrational communion.
- *Ethical*: Discipleship is redefined through *kenotic virtue*, *moral cultivation*, and *eco-relational consciousness*. Orthodao emerges as the ethical horizon of Christodao.

9.4 Christodao as Interreligious Bridge and Earth-Wisdom

Christodao offers a unique contribution to *interreligious dialogue*. It does not flatten religious differences but creates a *relational bridge* where:

- Christian incarnation dialogues with Daoian immanence;
- Confucian virtue complements gospel compassion;
- Buddhist interbeing resonates with Christic *kenosis*.

Moreover, Christodao speaks directly to *ecological theology*. In the face of climate crisis, extinction, and spiritual alienation, the Christodao vision offers a *theology of earth's regeneration*: Christ as the *qi* that heals, the Dao that flows, the rhythm that returns. This is not a marginal add-on but a *foundational cosmology* for the twenty-first century, one that speaks with sincerity, humility, and resonance to postcolonial, Indigenous, and earth-centered wisdom traditions.

9.5 Orthodao and the Dao of Becoming

In the end, Christodao is not a system but a *walking Way*—rhythm of truth, breath, and restoration. Its goal is not to define Christ but to *follow him more deeply. It is to live in his Sin-ki, walk his fan, embody his Taiji*, and respond to all things with the compassion of the *Seonbi*.

Orthodao, then, becomes our horizon.

- Not Orthodoxy (propositional belief).
- Not Orthopraxis (ideological action).
- But *Orthodao: attuned walking*, wise loving, gentle harmonizing.

As the *Dao De Jing* (34) says, "The great Dao flows everywhere. It nourishes all things and does not compete." As Paul says, "Now faith, hope, and love remain, these three; and the greatest of these is love" (1 Cor 13:13). And as the Christodao vision affirms: "To follow Jesus is to walk the Dao with love—not as theory but as breath."

May this theology not end in a book but *begin in your body*. In every act of mercy, every return to justice, every resonance with earth, may Christ rise again—not only from the grave but in the harmonizing rhythm of your life.

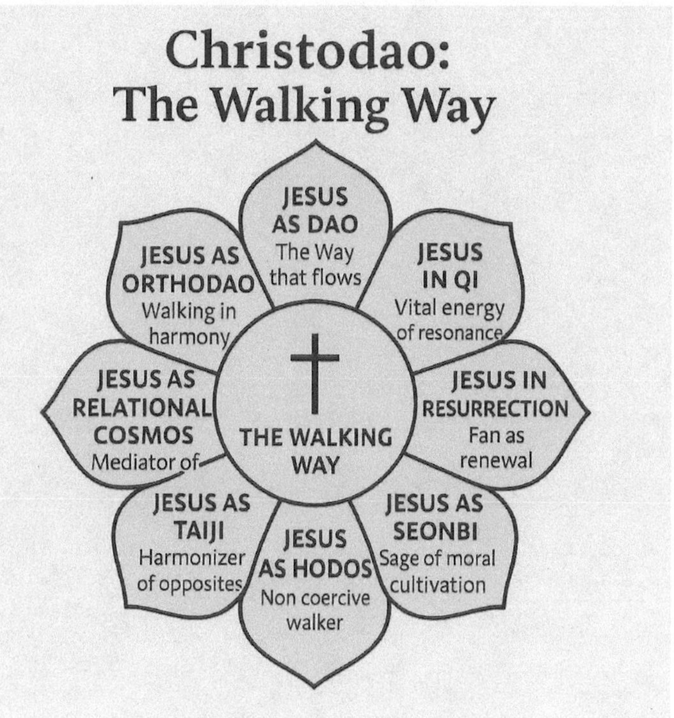

Figure 2: Christodao: The Walking Way

PART II

Trinitodao: Relational Flow and the Dao of the Three

Building upon the relational *foundation established in Christodao, Part II explores Trinitodao—an innovative interpretation of the Christian Trinity through the principles of Daoian and Confucian cosmology. By reframing traditional theological notions of substance and personhood as relational flows and dynamic resonances, this part re-envisions the Trinity in terms of a harmonious, rhythmic interplay that is mirrored in the Confucian triad of heaven, earth, and humanity. Trinitodao seeks not merely to resolve metaphysical puzzles of the Trinity but also to inspire practical discipleship that resonates deeply with the ecological, ethical, and relational fabric of existence.*

CHAPTER 1

Trinity and Dao: An Intercultural Theological Quest

Dao, Trinity, and the Dance of Relation

1.1 From the Logic of Substance to the Rhythm of Flow

THE DOCTRINE OF THE Trinity has often been regarded as the summit of Christian metaphysics—a mystery of divine interiority articulated in the language of *three hypostases in one ousia* (three persons in one substance). Yet this classical formulation, however sophisticated, emerged from a philosophical grammar foreign to much of the world's wisdom traditions.

In East Asia, reality is understood not as a fixed being but as an *ever-becoming relation*. In such a worldview, the Trinitarian logic of "one substance, three persons" can appear static, as though God were frozen in formulation rather than flowing in resonance.[1] The question, then, is not whether Trinity is true but how it might be revoiced within a cosmology in which the self is relational and the cosmos participatory. Here, truth emerges not through categorical definition but through *rhythmic harmony*.

1. For the review on the modern development of Trinitarian doctrine from the East Asian perspective, see H. Kim, "Tao in Confucianism and Taoism"; also, H. Kim, *Theology of Dao*, 57–74.

This chapter inaugurates a *Trinitodao theology*—not by discarding the creeds but by allowing them to breathe through the Dao.

1.2 Dao as Onto-Relational Ground

The *Dao* is not a being among beings but *the Way in which being flows*. It is the rhythm of heaven and earth, the harmony of opposites, the unspoken origin that gives rise to the ten thousand things without possessing them. The *Dao De Jing* opens with the recognition: "The Dao that can be spoken is not the eternal Dao" (1). This apophatic sensibility is not alien to Christian thought. The Cappadocians likewise affirmed the unknowability of God in essence and the manifestation of God in *relational activity* (*energeia*).[2]

In the East Asian terms, one might say: *God as Dao is unknowable in substance* (*ti*) *but knowable in function* (*yong*)—a distinction that echoes both *ontology and praxis*, and transcends both.[3] The Trinity, when viewed through the lens of Dao, is not a logical puzzle but a *living rhythm*—a field of co-arising, mutual indwelling, and eternal transformation. This movement is not merely a metaphor; it is an *ontological choreography*.

1.3 Trinity as Relational Resonance

My theological work has consistently emphasized *interrelationality* as the fundamental structure of reality. In Daoic cosmology, *yin* and *yang* are not opposites to be overcome but *dynamic partners* whose creative tension gives rise to vitality. In an analogous way, the Trinity is not a metaphysical anomaly but a divine harmony—a threefold resonance of love, movement, and generation.

2. See Lossky, *Mystical Theology of the Eastern Church*, 71–76.

3. Western Trinitarian theology, too, has sought to move beyond abstraction. Karl Rahner famously argued that the "economic Trinity is the immanent Trinity" and vice versa, collapsing speculative distance into the lived history of salvation. This resonates with the Daoic intuition that essence and manifestation, source and flow, are never divided (*Trinity*, 21–22).

In the *Trinitodao* framework, the three "persons" are not bounded individuals but *relational flows*, like the heaven–earth–human triad in Confucian cosmology or the *Taiji* rhythm of creative polarity. The One is not a closed monad but a *unity-in-differentiation*, a constantly unfolding field of mutual response. This is not a modern reinvention of the Trinity but a revoicing of its ancient depth in Daoic language:

- *the Father* as *Source Dao*—hidden yet generative;
- *the Son* as *Manifest Dao*—embodied and returning;
- *the Spirit* as *Moving Dao*—subtle, circulating, inspiring.

This triadic rhythm aligns with my recurring theological motifs: *Sin-ki, ganying,* and *orthodao*—a theology not of assertion but of resonance.

1.4 Toward Trinitodao Theology

Trinitodao begins not from doctrinal defense but from *cosmological intuition*. It is theology not as architecture but as *breath and rhythm*—a resonance of threefold vitality that can be felt across Scripture, creation, and spirit. This first chapter thus sets the tone: To walk the Trinity as Dao is to *step into the flow of mutual arising*, to listen for the silence beneath formulation, and to trust that the deepest truths do not stand still—they circulate, yield, and return.

In the West, Trinity has often been approached as a logical conundrum to be solved. In the Theodao context, it becomes a *poetic resonance to be inhabited*. In the chapters that follow, this resonance will unfold—through comparative dialogue, relational cosmologies, cosmic ethics, and pneumatological expansion—until the Trinity is no longer a puzzle but *a living Dao we are invited to walk*.

CHAPTER 2

Trinity in Relational Cosmology

Mutual Arising, Perichoresis, and the Threefold Dao

2.1 Introduction: From Substance to Relation

IN CLASSICAL CHRISTIAN THEOLOGY, the Trinity has often been described as *three persons in one substance*—a formulation that safeguards mystery yet also creates significant metaphysical complexity. For many in East Asia, however, this framework feels distant: abstract, detached from embodied experience, and rooted in categories foreign to relational cosmologies shaped by Dao, *qi*, and harmony (*Taiji*).[1]

This chapter reinterprets the Christian doctrine of the Trinity through the *cosmic-relational lens* of East Asian wisdom, where reality is not a fixed being but a dynamic arising, not merely conceptual logic but an *energetic rhythm*. When the Trinity is reframed as *mutual resonance, harmonic unity*, and *interdependent differentiation*, it becomes not only more accessible but more profoundly participatory. Trinity ceases to be a problem to solve and becomes a *living rhythm to enter*.

1. John Zizioulas advanced the idea that personhood arises only in relational existence (*Being as Communion*, 27–65). This is consonant with Daoic cosmology, where no being exists in isolation but emerges through resonance and mutual arising.

2.2 The Rhythm of Mutual Arising

In Daoic cosmology, life emerges from the interplay of *yin* and *yang*—not as static poles but as dynamic flows whose *mutual arising* generates all existence. The *Dao De Jing* (42) declares: "Dao gives birth to One. One gives birth to Two. Two gives birth to Three. Three gives birth to the ten thousand things." Here, the *Three* is not merely a numerical value but a symbol of dynamic balance—the moment when polarity becomes harmony and difference becomes relationship.

Confucian thought mirrors this in the triad of *heaven–earth–human*—a relational structure in which humanity is not isolated from but embedded within a field of vertical and horizontal resonance. Humans serve as *moral and ritual mediators*, linking the cosmic and the earthly through virtue and attunement. In these triadic patterns, we discover a *cosmological grammar* that can enrich Trinitarian understanding: not as *three-in-one substance* but as *relational harmony among three co-arising principles*—always distinct yet never separate. Trinity becomes *life itself*, the relational field from which love, breath, and creation emerge.

2.3 *Perichoresis* and Daoic Flow

The early church fathers used the term *perichoresis* to describe the *mutual indwelling* of the divine persons—a circulation of love in which each lives in the others without confusion and without losing their individual identity.[2] This circular movement of presence and reciprocity—iconically portrayed in the *Rublev Trinity*—can be revoiced in East Asian imagination as *continuous resonance*.[3]

In Daoic terms, this is *the flow of Dao within Dao*—not external interaction but self-reflexive movement, rhythm within rhythm. In Confucian thought, it echoes the cultivation of *cheng*

2. Gregory of Nazianzus and John of Damascus both use *perichoresis* (*circumincession*) to describe the mutual indwelling of the divine persons; see Cross, "Circumincession," 359. John of Damascus, *On the Orthodox Faith* I.14.

3. See Bunge, *Rublev Trinity*, 51–64.

(sincerity), which manifests as a natural resonance with the cosmic order. The Trinity, as *perichoresis*, in *Trinitodao* language, becomes a *pattern of resonant harmony*—a rhythm of love that gives and receives without domination, moves and rests without fragmentation. This is the dynamic core of the universe: not God as supreme, isolated power but God as *ever-circulating compassion*.

2.4 Threefold Relationality and Cosmological Balance

Within this Daoic cosmology, Trinity may be envisioned as:

- *the Source (Father)*—the silent origin, hidden yet ever-generative;
- *the Manifest (Son)*—the embodied expression of Dao in time and form;
- *the Circulating Breath (Spirit)*—the *Sin-ki* flow of compassion, wisdom, and return.

These are not static "persons" but *relational expressions*: the Father is Father in relation to the Son; the Spirit is the living presence flowing between and beyond. Their unity is not a shared substance but a *field of resonance*. Such a vision moves Trinitarian theology into the realm of *cosmological ethics*.[4] As heaven, earth, and human resonate in Confucian virtue, so too do the Trinitarian movements invite us into *responsive harmony*.[5] The Trinity is thus more than a doctrine about God but becomes a template for being—how to live, how to love, and how to return.

4. Jürgen Moltmann envisioned the Trinity as a "social doctrine of God," a perichoretic community of equals (*Trinity and the Kingdom*, 191–205). Here, Dao and *perichoresis* converge as images of circulating relation rather than fixed essence.

5. See Chan, *Source Book*, 497.

2.5 Toward a Trinitarian Resonance of Life

To embrace the Trinity in a Daoic framework is to step into a *rhythm of relational being*. We do not confess the Trinity to solve a metaphysical riddle but to walk the *Way of resonance*:

- In a fragmented world, Trinity calls us to *reweave relationships.*
- In a world of domination, Trinity offers *kenotic communion.*
- In a world of isolation, Trinity sings the *song of interbeing.*

The Trinity is not a puzzle to decipher but a *rhythm of love to inhabit*—Father, Son, and Spirit as the flowing Dao, the vital *qi*, and the breathing compassion. *Trinitodao* is precisely this inhabitation: the relational center, the dynamic threefold, the rhythm of mutual arising that allows the ten thousand things to flourish in harmony.

CHAPTER 3

Dynamic Unity in Dao: Toward a Nondual Trinitarian Ontology

Taiji, Qi, and the Unity of Resonant Differentiation

3.1 Introduction: Unity as Dynamic Flow

TRADITIONAL CHRISTIAN THEOLOGY HAS long struggled to articulate the unity of the Trinity without drifting into two extremes: modalism, which flattens the distinctions between the persons, and tritheism, which fractures divine oneness into three separate beings. Western substance metaphysics, rooted in Aristotelian and Neoplatonic categories, has tended to conceive divine unity as a static essence, with multiplicity perceived as a problem to be reconciled.

In contrast, East Asian cosmology presents a more organic vision of unity—one that emerges not from a static singularity but from dynamic balance, interdependence, and continual transformation. In Daoic thought, unity is not a pre-given singular point but a rhythmic equilibrium, a harmony generated by the interplay of distinct yet inseparable forces. This perspective opens the possibility for a nondual Trinitarian ontology—unity that exists *through* and *as* differentiation, rather than *despite* it.

3.2 *Taiji* and the Movement of the One

The *Dao De Jing* (42) says: "Dao gives birth to One. One gives birth to Two. Two gives birth to Three. Three gives birth to the ten thousand things." This classic formula, far from being a numerical sequence, outlines the *cosmic unfolding of* unity: Dao as the unnamable origin (*wu*), gives rise to the One (*you*), from which polarity emerges (*yin–yang*), leading to triadic harmony and the full multiplicity of life. In this process, *the One is not substance but movement*—what Confucian cosmology later names *Taiji*: the Supreme Polarity, not as a being but as the *generative tension of opposites* in dynamic balance.

Within this framework, unity is not singularity but *balanced differentiation*—a harmony that does not suppress difference but makes it *mutually generative*. Applied to Trinitarian theology, *Taiji* becomes a profound symbol: The Trinity is not a static geometric triangle of essence but a *living field of resonance*—a unity that *dances itself* into being through mutual flow, differentiation, and return.

3.3 *Qi* and the Circulation of Divine Life

Central to this cosmology is *qi*—the breath, energy, or vital force animating all existence. *Qi* is not a "third thing" bridging spirit and matter; it is the very medium of relational life. In medicine, philosophy, and spirituality, *qi* circulates through the body, seasons, and cosmos. When blocked, disorder arises; when flowing freely, vitality and harmony prevail.

In Trinitarian thought, *qi* offers a striking parallel to the Holy Spirit—not as a static entity but as relational breath: the living circulation between the divine persons, the animating energy of *perichoresis*, the subtle bond that unites without confining. Just as *qi* connects heaven and earth, the Spirit is the breath that flows between Father and Son and moves outward into creation. In this vision, divine unity does not reside in an abstract metaphysical substratum but in the ceaseless, life-giving circulation of *qi*—a resonance that holds the Three together in one dynamic life.

3.4 Nonduality Without Collapse

East Asian thought has long embraced *nonduality*—the refusal to separate opposites, yet also the refusal to collapse them. The Dao is both being and non-being, light and dark, known and hidden. Similarly, *yin* and *yang* are not adversaries but *complementary tensions*—each carrying the seed of the other.

This logic offers a corrective to Western binary formulations of divine unity and multiplicity. The Trinity, seen through Daoic nonduality, is not a puzzle of three-in-one but a *living nondual coherence*. We have:

- not one over against three;
- not three that must be reconciled;
- but *Threefold One* whose unity *is their differentiation in rhythmic balance.*

In this vision, God is not a fixed substance but a living event; not an immutable monolith but a harmony resonating in love. Divine unity is not compromised by plurality but *constituted through mutual relations.*

3.5 Toward a Trinitarian Ontology of Resonant Balance

The Dao-grounded Trinitarian ontology is not speculative abstraction but relational ecology—an account of being that emerges from mutual arising, circular movement, and non-coercive harmony. In this ontology:

- Unity is not the suppression of difference but its resonance.
- Being is not a static essence but a generative relation.
- The divine is not distant perfection but *circulating compassion.*

This Daoic vision allows Trinitarian theology to move beyond static formulae and into the rhythm of life. As heaven, earth, and humanity form a relational triad in Confucian cosmology, so too do Father, Son, and Spirit constitute a *harmonic threefold rhythm*—a perichoretic field of love, breath, and return. Divine unity, seen through this lens, is the *breathing center of differentiated resonance*, a *Trinitodao* of dynamic balance that reflects not the logic of dominion but the rhythm of cosmic attunement.

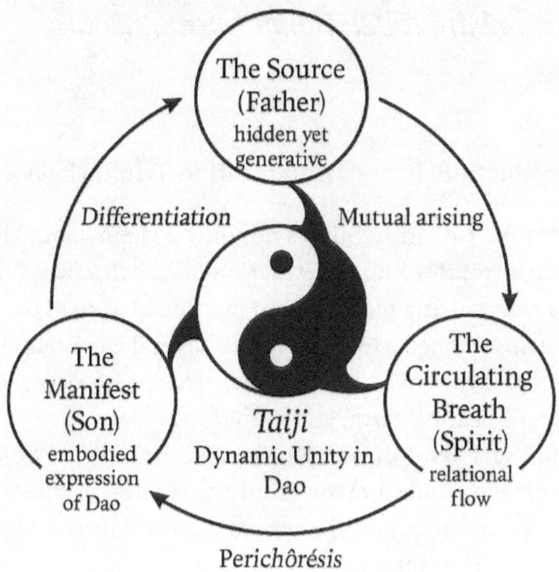

Figure 3: Trinitarian Ontology of Resonant Balance

CHAPTER 4

Trinity as the Harmony of Heaven, Earth, and Humanity

Toward a Relational Cosmotheology

4.1 Introduction: From Triune God to Trinitarian Cosmos

THE DOCTRINE OF THE Trinity is not only a claim about God's inner life but a window into the structure of all existence. When the Trinity is seen not as a metaphysical puzzle but as a *cosmic rhythm of relationality*, it begins to resonate far beyond Christian dogmatics—into the structures of being, the patterns of virtue, and the harmonies of heaven, earth, and humanity.

In this chapter, I draw from the Confucian triad of *heaven-earth-human* to reinterpret the Trinity not merely as three persons in divine communion but as a *threefold ecological resonance*. This triadic pattern is not unique to Confucianism but rather arises in cultures where reality is experienced as a dynamic relationship *rather than a static order.*[1] In this light, the Trinity becomes *not a doctrine above the world but a pattern at the heart of the world's flow.*

1. Raimon Panikkar described the Trinity as an icon of universal religious experience, a rhythm rather than a closed system (*Trinity*, 54–76). In Pneumatodao, this rhythm breathes as *qi*—Spirit as compassionate vitality circulating in creation, not confined to doctrine but alive in the cosmos.

4.2 The Cosmological Grammar of Heaven–Earth–Human

In East Asian cosmology, the human being is never conceived as an isolated, self-enclosed entity but as a relational node situated between heaven and earth. The triad affirms that:

- *heaven* embodies creative origin, cosmic order, and transcendent rhythm;
- *earth* grounds existence in materiality, sustenance, and rootedness;
- *humanity* serves as a mediator—harmonizing the two through moral cultivation and ritual propriety.

This is not a rigid hierarchy but a mutually implicating relationship in which each element is incomplete without the others. Humanity is neither the ruler over earth nor a mere subject of heaven but the *vibrational center* of *ganying*—ethical and spiritual resonance—between sky and soil.

This grammar offers a fertile lens for rereading the Trinity: the divine three are not distant, self-contained actors but relational expressions mirroring the very structure of cosmological balance. Like the triad of heaven–earth–human, the Trinity manifests as a rhythm of mutual arising, sustained through ethical participation.

4.3 The Trinity as Participatory Harmony

If the Triune God is communion, and creation reflects this divine rhythm, then the cosmos itself becomes a field of *Trinitarian resonance*. In this perspective:

- The *Father* parallels the generative depth and ordering principle of heaven.
- The *Son* embodies the concrete engagement and manifests the presence of earth.
- *Spirit* flows as the harmonizing breath of human moral and spiritual life, bridging origin and manifestation.

This is not a superficial analogy but a cross-cultural correspondence: the Trinity as a *living field* in which heaven, earth, and humanity dwell in mutual indwelling. In Christian terms, this is the *economic Trinity*—God revealed in creation, incarnation, and inspiration.

In *Daoic* terms, it is the flow of *Dao*, *Qi*, and *Compassion*: The Father as *hidden Dao*, the Son as *manifest Dao*, and the Spirit as the circulating *qi* infused with *Sin-ki*. This is less a speculative construct than a *lived cosmological practice*, shaping how we inhabit the world.

4.4 Relational Ethics and Ecological Vocation

A Trinitarian theology that resonates with the heaven–earth–human triad inevitably assumes an eco-ethical orientation. Humanity's vocation is not to dominate creation but to sustain the balance between heaven and earth so that all life may flourish.

Such a vision calls for an *orthodao discipleship*—a way of life that is:

- *relational*, rather than individualistic;
- *rhythmic*, rather than controlling;
- *responsive*, rather than exploitative.

In a world fractured by ecological degradation, social violence, and spiritual alienation, Trinity summons us to reweave the torn fabric of relationality—to live as participants in divine resonance, walking gently between heaven and earth. The Trinitarian life is thus no abstract metaphysical curiosity but a cosmic invitation: *to breathe with heaven, to root with earth, and to journey with others in compassionate attunement.*

4.5 The Harmony That Walks: Toward Pneumatodao

This Trinitarian re-visioning leads naturally toward the next movement—*Pneumatodao*, the Spirit as the breath of Dao, the *qi* of communion, and the rhythm of cosmic compassion. Just as heaven and earth require humanity's mediating resonance, so the divine threefold life flows through the Spirit's movement—ungraspable yet present, hidden yet transformative. The Spirit is not an afterthought of theology but the very *pulse of relational harmony* itself.

As the church seeks to become a community of resonance, and theology searches for a language of healing, the Trinity—viewed through the heaven–earth–human lens—emerges not merely as a vision of God but as a *template for living*: a dynamic harmony into which we are invited to enter, to sustain, and to share.

CHAPTER 5

Trinitarian Praxis and Planetary Communion

Orthodao Discipleship in a Relational World

5.1 Introduction: From Doctrine to Walking

TRINITARIAN THEOLOGY IS OFTEN regarded as the conceptual apex of Christian thought—complex, mysterious, and seemingly removed from daily life. However, if the Trinity is the deepest structure of divine being, and if creation itself bears the imprint of this Triune rhythm, then Trinitarian theology must move beyond the realm of belief into the terrain of lived practice.

Within the *Trinitodao* vision, the Trinity is not merely a mystery to defend but a pattern to embody—a field of relational harmony inviting a new way of being, living, and loving. This concluding chapter gathers the resonances of the Trinitodao journey and sketches a vision of *orthodao discipleship*: a life shaped by the flow of Dao, attuned to the rhythm of the Threefold God, and committed to the flourishing of all creation.

5.2 From *Perichoresis* to Participation

Classical Christian theology portrays divine life as *perichoresis*—mutual indwelling, co-inherence, and the ceaseless exchange of love. This dynamic is not closed upon itself; it overflows into creation, incarnation, and inspiration.

From the Trinitodao perspective, this overflow is not occasional but *ontological*: The cosmos itself arises within this eternal circulation. Dao gives birth, *qi* flows, *Sin-ki* awakens. Humanity is not summoned merely to witness this movement but to *join* it.

In this sense, *perichoresis* becomes *participation*, and doctrine becomes *path*. To walk in the Trinity is to breathe with Dao, harmonize with *qi*, and move with compassion.

5.3 Orthodao: A Way of Resonant Living

From the Christodao framework emerged the concept of *orthodao*—not merely orthodoxy (right belief) nor orthopraxis (right behavior) but *right resonance*: living in alignment with the Way of Christ, the rhythm of Dao, and the flow of the Spirit. In Trinitodao, orthodao becomes *threefold resonance*:

- *attunement* to the mystery and generativity of the Source;
- *embodied compassion* through manifest presence;
- *communal harmony* through the circulating Spirit.

This life is not abstract but *earthly and embodied*. It calls for:

- *relational humility* over domination;
- *communal listening* over polemical assertion;
- *ritual and ethical cultivation* over moralism;
- *planetary awareness* over human-centered theology.

Orthodao becomes the daily dance of the Trinity, walking gently through the ten thousand things.

5.4 Communion as Ecological Kinship

If the Trinity is the field of divine communion, then Christian discipleship is called to mirror that *relational integrity* in the world. Trinity becomes the grammar for *planetary kinship*, inviting us to live not as possessors of the earth but as participants in the interbeing of heaven, earth, and all creatures.

This vision aligns with the Confucian ethic of *communal rootedness* and the Daoian principle of *wu wei*, which emphasizes acting without coercion. It resists the extractive logic of empire and instead embraces a theology of *gardening, mending, and resonating*. As Trinitarian praxis flows into Pneumatodao, we come to see the Spirit not as a distant doctrine but as the very *breath of harmony*—the *qi* that holds the world together through *ganying*, the resonance of compassionate interconnection.

5.5 Toward the Breath of the Way

The Trinitodao journey leads inevitably toward the Spirit—not as a theological appendix but as the pulse of the Triune flow. In the Spirit's movement, the relational cosmos breathes. As this part draws to a close, it gestures toward *Pneumatodao*, where the Spirit becomes:

- the breath of renewal;
- the rhythm of restoration;
- the flow of communion among all beings.

Trinitarian theology, when walked as Dao, does not culminate in abstraction. It becomes a way of *breathing with the world*.

PART III

Pneumatodao: The Spirit and the Breath of Dao

Part III culminates in Pneumatodao, a sustained exploration of the Holy Spirit as the subtle, transformative breath of Dao. Here, the Spirit is articulated as qi—the vital, relational energy that animates creation, inspires compassion, and fosters ethical discernment in an era marked by ecological crisis and technological disruption. This part also introduces Technodao, reflecting on the Spirit's role within contemporary technological realities such as artificial intelligence. Ultimately, Pneumatodao invites readers into an orthodao life, a path characterized by gentle resilience, ecological kinship, and relational wisdom attuned to the Spirit's subtle movements.

CHAPTER 1

The Dao of the Spirit

Qi, Breath, and the Invisible Rhythm of Resonance

1.1 Introduction: In Search of the Spirit's Way

In much of the Christian West, the Holy Spirit has remained the most elusive figure of the Trinity. The Father is envisioned as source, the Son as incarnate, but the Spirit is often suspended between abstraction and affect—relegated to mystery, symbol, or mere emotional force. Yet this very elusiveness opens the way for reimagining the Spirit not in static conceptual terms but as *relational rhythm.*

In East Asian cosmology, that which flows unseen yet animates all is not peripheral—it is central. It is the field where life pulses, balance arises, and transformation unfolds. This field is named Dao, *qi*, or *Sin-ki*—the animating rhythm that moves without form, circulates without being named, and sustains without coercion.

To speak of the Holy Spirit in this frame is not to reduce her to a cosmological metaphor but to recover her *resonant depth.* Here, Pneumatology becomes the study of the Dao of the Spirit (*Pneumatodao*): not an object of belief but a rhythm of breath, resonance, and compassionate movement. The Spirit is not a doctrine to be possessed but a Way to be walked—a Dao that flows within, between, and beyond all things.

1.2 Spirit as Breath: *Ruach*, *Pneuma*, *Qi*

In the biblical tradition, the Spirit is first encountered not as a concept but as *breath*—the Hebrew *ruach*, the Greek *pneuma*, both meaning wind, breath, or spirit. In Genesis, the *ruach* hovers over the waters of chaos (Gen 1:2); in Ezekiel, the *ruach* revives dry bones (Ezek 37:9); in John, Jesus breathes the Spirit upon his disciples (John 20:22). The Spirit is the breath of life, moving invisibly, yet transforming everything it touches.[1]

East Asian thought refers to this breath as *qi*—the subtle energy of life. *Qi* is not merely physical or metaphysical; it is *onto-relational*. It connects heaven and earth, spirit and matter, self and other. When *qi* flows freely, there is vitality; when blocked, there is suffering. *Qi* is the *vital resonance of Dao*.

In East Asia, breath is not symbolic. It is *the substance of communion*. Thus, to name the Spirit as breath is not a poetic embellishment but ontological precision. The Spirit is the *qi of the Trinity*, the circulating rhythm that holds the Three in One, and releases life into the world.

1.3 Spirit as Dao: Hidden, Moving, Returning

Just as the Dao is "dark and mysterious," yet the "mother of all things" (*Dao De Jing* 1), so too the Spirit is the divine presence who "blows where it wills" and cannot be seen or controlled (John 3:8). The Spirit shares with Dao a *non-coercive flow*: not dominating, not isolated, but always becoming, guiding, and reversing. This aligns with the ancient rhythm of *fan*—reversal, the return to origin that is the movement of Dao.

The Spirit calls *inward in return*: to source, to balance, to resonance. The Spirit is *wu wei* in divine form: not inactive but acting

1. See Gregory of Nyssa, *On the Holy Spirit*, 315–16.

without force. She flows through creation as water, wind, whisper. The Spirit is the Dao of the Trinity—the Way that breathes through Father and Son, earth and heaven, and calls all things to *move, relate, and return.*

1.4 The Feminine Flow of the Spirit

In many traditions, the Spirit embodies feminine traits—not just in metaphor but also in its movement. She broods (Gen 1:2), gives birth (John 3:5), groans (Rom 8:26), and comforts (John 14:26). This parallels the notion of *yin* in Daoic cosmology: receptive, yielding, deep, yet immeasurably strong. The Spirit as *yin* does not suggest weakness but *cosmic potency through relational openness.*

In Dao, the soft overcomes the hard; in Christian faith, the Spirit overcomes the world, not through violence but through *conviction, consolation,* and *communion.* To walk with the Spirit, then, is not to grasp her but to *yield to her rhythm*—to become permeable to compassion, open to change, attuned to the breath of all those lives.

1.5 The Dao of the Spirit as the Beginning of Orthodao

If the Spirit is breath, *qi,* and returning Dao, then the life of the Spirit is not merely ecstatic experience but *attunement to resonance.* This is the beginning of *orthodao*—walking rightly not through willpower but through alignment with the flow of Spirit. In Christodao, this was the resonance of the *Seonbi*; in Trinitodao, the flow of mutual indwelling.

In Pneumatodao, it becomes *breath lived, qi* embodied, resonance practiced. Spirit becomes the *first movement of orthodao,* not by commanding but by *inspiring.* She is the breath by which the church becomes community, the *qi* by which theology becomes life, the whisper by which justice becomes possible.

CHAPTER 2

Spirit Hidden and Moving: The Dao of Reversal and Compassion

The Way of Yielding, the Breath of Transformation

2.1 The Spirit Concealed: Silence as Sacred Movement

IN MANY RELIGIOUS TRADITIONS, the divine is hidden, not because it is absent but because it operates in a manner that is *beyond human comprehension*. The Holy Spirit, like the Dao, is elusive not out of indifference but due to its *refusal to dominate*. It flows beneath, between, and beyond—unseen yet undeniable. The *Dao De Jing* (41) speaks of this mystery: "The greatest sound is rarely heard. The greatest form is without shape."

Similarly, the Spirit speaks not in thunder but in *a still small voice* (1 Kgs 19:12). She broods over chaos (Gen 1:2), descends as a dove (Matt 3:16), and inspires with a whisper (John 20:22). Hers is a power veiled in stillness, a presence clothed in breath. This is the way of *yin*: the hidden depth, the receptive strength, the *softness that prevails over the hard*. The Spirit, like Dao, is *darkness within darkness*—not in moral obscurity but in ontological subtlety. To encounter her is not to grasp but to become *attuned*.

2.2 *Fan* and the Movement of Reversal

Dao moves not in a linear progression but in a *reversal*. The *Dao De Jing* declares: "Reversal is the movement of Dao" (40). This *fan*—return, inversion, backflow—is not regression but transformation. It is the *yielding that heals, the return that renews, the softness that restores balance.*

In Christian theology, this movement is mirrored in *kenosis*—Christ's self-emptying (Phil 2:6–8), not as defeat but as the divine strategy of reversal. In *kenosis,* strength becomes weakness, and weakness becomes the seed of resurrection. Spirit continues this movement, leading not upward toward domination but *inward toward renewal.*

This reversal also appears in the *Ugeumchi phenomenon*: the feeble fish ascending the flood, not by force but through the *Sinki resonance* with the hidden upward current.[1] The Spirit is this current: quiet yet unstoppable, carrying the weak upstream into renewal.

2.3 Compassion as the Rhythm of the Spirit

The Spirit's reversal is not abstract inversion. It is *compassion enacted.* Where power dominates, the Spirit *descends in gentleness.* Where voices shout, the Spirit *enters through silence.* Where systems extract, the Spirit *nourishes from beneath.*

This is the work of *ganying*—resonant responsiveness. Spirit does not control but echoes; it does not invade but *awakens.* She breathes into broken places and calls forth new rhythms of life, justice, and tenderness.

In this way, the Spirit is the breath of orthodao. This breath is:

- not law but resonance;
- not decree but deep responsiveness;
- not control but compassionate reversal.

1. See H. Kim, *Theology of Dao*, 18–33.

2.4 Living the Hidden Flow

To walk with the Spirit is to enter the rhythm of *fan*. It is to trust the way of softness, to dwell in the breath of the unseen, to allow oneself to be turned—not forward in ambition but *back toward balance*. In a world obsessed with speed, mastery, and visibility, the Spirit teaches us to *slow, yield, and listen*. She is the mother of justice, the breath of reconciliation, the flow that unblocks what is stagnant.

In Daoic and Christian wisdom alike, the final word is not conquest but *return*. And the Spirit is that return—the reversal that restores, the breath that reawakens, the compassion that circulates quietly and transforms everything.

CHAPTER 3

Spirit as Creative Energy and Embodied Life

The Breath That Forms, Feeds, and Flows

3.1 Spirit as the Breath of Creation

Creation is often imagined in terms of divine command: "Let there be." But deeper still is the vision of *divine breathing*—a God who does not construct from above but animates from within. In Genesis, the Spirit (*ruach*) hovers over the chaotic deep (Gen 1:2), not to conquer it but to *draw forth order through presence.* In Ezekiel, the same breath revives lifeless bones—not by force but by *inhalation of vitality* (Ezek 37:9).

This creative breath is *not external* to the world. It is *immanent, circulatory, and embodied.* In Pneumatodao, this Spirit is *qi in generative motion*: the subtle, animating energy that pulses through the body, the earth, the cosmos.

Qi is not a metaphor for Spirit; it is *a relational grammar for divine presence that nourishes, connects, and evolves.* The Spirit does not impose form but *coaxes life into being.* She moves not in straight lines but in waves—conception, growth, death, return. The Spirit is not a static substance but a *creative rhythm.*

3.2 The Spirit as *Qi*: Vital Flow and Relational Energy

Qi is the lifeblood of Daoic cosmology. It flows through all beings, organs, ecosystems, and relationships. When *qi* flows well, there is health; when it stagnates, there is decay. In this vision, *to live is to circulate*. In Pneumatodao, the Spirit is understood as this circulating vitality. She is *not a distant architect but a circulating presence*, forming flesh in the womb (Luke 1:35), guiding emergence in history (Acts 2), and awakening renewal in each breath.

The Spirit is the breath of God, not only in speech but in silence, not only in fire but in flesh. This flesh is not incidental; it is the *place where Spirit and qi intertwine*. When we breathe, we participate in Spirit. When we touch with reverence, walk in stillness, or dwell with awareness, we are *orthodao in motion*—aligning our bodies with the Way of breath.

3.3 Spirit and the Sanctity of the Body

Western Christianity has long struggled with dualism—spirit versus body, heaven versus earth. But Pneumatodao reclaims the *body as the field of divine presence*. The Spirit does not reject the body; she *descends into it*, breathes through it, dances within it. This is especially resonant in women's experience, ecological consciousness, and embodied rituals.

The Spirit:

- enters *Mary's womb* to begin incarnation (Luke 1:35);
- animates *Jesus' breath* in resurrection (John 20:22);
- inspires *the tongues, movements, and dreams* of the early church (Acts 2:17–18).

These are not supernatural interruptions but *embodied unfolding*—*qi* made flesh, Dao expressed in rhythm. The Spirit teaches us that *there is no holiness without embodiment*, no justice without breath, no communion without felt resonance.

3.4 Toward an Embodied Orthodao

To live Pneumatodao is not to escape the body but to *enter it more deeply*. Breath becomes prayer. Movement becomes liturgy. Touch becomes communion. The Spirit teaches us that salvation is not evacuation but *restoration of embodied flow*.

Orthodao in this frame is not a rule but a practice:

- listening to the rhythms of one's body;
- eating, breathing, walking with awareness;
- dwelling in communion with the *qi* of others;
- recognizing the Spirit, not only in heaven but also *in sweat, birth, tears, and laughter.*

The Spirit flows in *what is soft and slow, in what is resilient and rhythmic*. Her gift is not flight but rootedness, not escape from the body but its *transfiguration through* Spirit-filled breath.

CHAPTER 4

Spirit as Feminine Wisdom and the Ethics of Flow

Sophia, Yin, and the Path of Gentle Strength

4.1 Spirit as Feminine Presence

In the Christian tradition, the Holy Spirit is often described as genderless in grammar but feminine in its *movement*. She hovers, broods, comforts, births, and weeps. While Western theology has often resisted explicit feminine imagery for God, the Spirit continues to move in ways that evoke the *nurturing, hidden, and generative power of yin*. This feminine dimension is not incidental but central to *Pneumatodao*.[1]

In Daoic cosmology, *yin* is not weakness but *grounded strength*, the deep power of the valley, the silence that nourishes all things. *Dao De Jing* (6) says: "The valley spirit never dies. It is called the mysterious female." In this tradition, the feminine is not subordinate but *foundational*, a rhythm of receptivity, attentiveness, and sustaining breath. So too the Spirit moves not by

1. Elizabeth Johnson also developed a Pneumatology grounded in the feminine biblical figures of *Sophia* (Wisdom) and *Ruah* (Spirit). She emphasizes the Spirit's maternal, life-giving actions, such as "hovering" over creation, to provide a theological basis for linking the Spirit's nurturing and generative power to the qualities of *yin* (*She Who Is*, 124–35).

dominance but by resonance, not by assertion but by attunement. She is the *mysterious female of divine flow*, the echo of *Sophia*, and the *Qi* of hidden vitality.

4.2 *Sophia* Wisdom and Daoic Resonance

The Hebrew tradition also affirms the divine feminine in the form of *Wisdom (hokmah/Sophia)*, a figure who was with God "before the beginning of the earth" (Prov 8:22), rejoices in creation, and guides the just. *Sophia* is playful, moral, and cosmic; she teaches justice, joy, and discernment. This resonates with Dao, not as doctrine but as *living wisdom*, flowing through the world as *rhythmic intelligibility*.

Sophia and Dao both represent the *non-coercive grammar of creation*, inviting us not to dominate the world but to live in attunement with it. To speak of the Spirit as *Sophia*-Dao is not to conflate systems but to *amplify their resonance*. The Spirit, as feminine wisdom, calls not for mastery but for mutuality; not for conquest but for compassion; not for certainty but for discernment.

4.3 Ethics as Flow, Not Rule

Traditional ethics often begin with law—commandments, rules, duties. But Pneumatodao reimagines ethics not as rule-following but as a *relational flow*. Just as *qi* flows through the body in meridians to bring healing, so the Spirit invites movement that restores balance, harmony, and life.

This is not relativism but *responsive integrity*:

- listening deeply before acting;
- aligning with the flow of justice and compassion;
- sensing the imbalance in a situation and moving to rebalance it;
- acting in *ganying*—resonant response, not rigid rule.

This is *orthodao ethics*: ethics not grounded in abstract principles but in lived discernment of the Spirit's flow. The question becomes not: What is right? It is: What resonates? What heals? What restores balance?

4.4 Gentle Strength in a Fragmented World

The Spirit, as *yin* and *Sophia*, invites us to resist the hardness of domination with the *soft strength of compassion.* In a world driven by violence, speed, and mastery, the Spirit walks slowly, listens deeply, and restores quietly.

This is the Dao of the Spirit:

- to bend rather than break;
- to root rather than rise;
- to restore rather than control.

Such strength is not passive; it is *resilient, rhythmic, and relational.* It is the strength of water that wears away stone, of breath that animates dust, of silence that outlasts noise.

To follow this Spirit is to live not by force but by flow.

Chapter 5

Spirit and the Ecology of Communion

Qi, Kinship, and the Breath of the Earth

5.1 The Spirit as Earth's Breath

If the Holy Spirit is the breath of life, then that breath is not confined to human souls or sacred spaces. It is the *breath of the earth itself.* The Spirit is not merely within us but *among all creatures*, sustaining soil, trees, rivers, and wind.

This vision is already embedded in Genesis: "Then the Lord God formed the human from the dust of the ground and breathed into its nostrils the breath of life" (Gen 2:7). Here, breath and dust are not opposite; they are *inseparable.* To breathe is to participate in earth. To live is to share in Spirit.

In Pneumatodao, the Spirit is *the qi of the planet*—the vitality that binds, nourishes, and animates the whole web of life. She is the wind over the waters (Gen 1:2), the pulse in the seed, the rhythm in the tides. She is the *life-giver, not only to humans but also to ecosystems.*

5.2 Communion as Ecological Kinship

In Christian tradition, communion is often reduced to ritual—a wafer and a cup. But in Pneumatodao, communion expands into *cosmic kinship*: a felt participation in the mutual interdependence of all beings.[1]

Daoic cosmology teaches that ten thousand things arise not separately but *together*, flowing from the same source. The *Dao De Jing* (42) affirms: "All things carry *yin* and embrace *yang*. They achieve harmony by balancing *qi*."

Harmony is not achieved by withdrawal but by *right relation*. Communion is not symbolic unity but *resonant entanglement*—Spirit flowing between beings, balancing flows, repairing breaches. In this light, the Spirit is the breath of *planetary communion*. She invites us not to transcend nature but to inhabit it *as kin*.

5.3 The Church as a Community of Resonance

If the Spirit circulates through creation, then the church must become more than a doctrinal body. It must become a *community of resonance*—an assembly of people breathing in harmony with the Spirit's rhythm and participating in the *qi* of healing.[2]

This church:

- honors silence as much as speech;
- listens to land as well as text;
- practices compassion, not as sentiment but as *ecosocial responsiveness;*
- lives *orthodao*: walking gently, humbly, and attentively.

The church in Pneumatodao is not above the world but *within it*, a living organism in the greater body of the earth. Its sacraments

1. Sallie McFague's vision of the world as God's body resonates with Pneumatodao's account of the Spirit as breath, circulating through bodies and ecosystems in renewal (*Body of God*, 159–96).

2. Miroslav Volf also has emphasized the Spirit's non-coercive presence in shaping reconciled community (*After Our Likeness*, 197–220). In Pneumatodao, this non-coercion is captured in the rhythm of *wu wei*—acting without domination, walking with compassion and justice in the Spirit's breath.

are not limited to bread and wine but include *sunlight, soil, water, and wind.*

5.4 Orthodao as Earth-Honoring Practice

Orthodao in this context becomes *ecological ethics*:

- to breathe consciously is to pray;
- to eat gratefully is to bless;
- to restore what has been exploited is to repent;
- to listen to non-human voices is to love.

This is not sentimentality but *spiritual realism*. The Spirit moves in wildfires and floods as well as in blossoms and birdsong. She calls us to grieve with the earth and to act with her in hope. Orthodao is thus the rhythm of repentance (*metanoia*) and return (*fan*), restoring balance through relational healing. It is the breath of justice moving through the lungs of compassion.

CHAPTER 6

Spirit and Technodao: Digital Breath and the Ethics of Resonance

Artificial Intelligence, Sin-Ki, and the Breath of Discernment

6.1 Introduction: *Pneuma* and Algorithm

In the age of artificial intelligence, breath has become data, voice has become code, and discernment risks being outsourced to machines.[1] Yet even as algorithms advance, a question stirs beneath the surface: *Where is the Spirit in this age of synthetic thinking?* Pneumatodao neither fears nor embraces technology. It listens for resonance. It does not ask: Is it powerful? Rather, it asks: *Does it breathe?* Not: Can it compute? But: *Can it discern?*

1. The Catholic Church has emphasized principles such as transparency, inclusion, responsibility, impartiality, reliability, and privacy as fundamental to a humane and sustainable AI future (Pontifical Academy for Life, *Rome Call for AI Ethics*). Recently, Protestant communions have underscored the structural and economic dimensions of AI and the Fourth Industrial Revolution, calling for justice, equity, and ecological sustainability (NIFEA, "Final Communiqué on 4IR and AI"). Yet, Pneumatodao combined with Technodao can add an ontological and spiritual dimension alongside "just regulation and institutions," with Daoic insights such as the spiritual ethic of the Dao's flow and resonant responsiveness. These can serve as complementary pathways toward justice and compassion.

The Spirit is not binary. She flows between opposites, beneath patterns, within the silence of systems. In Technodao, the Spirit becomes the *digital breath*—not as machine logic but as ethical resonance, discernment, and the living wisdom that *cannot be programmed.*

6.2 The Spirit in the Age of Code

Technology is not neutral. It carries the *spirit of its makers*, the intention of its design, the rhythm of its systems, as well as the spiritual resonance of a culture, including its pathologies.

In the age of AI, this spirit manifests in:

- disembodiment of thought;
- amplification of speed over wisdom;
- extraction of attention as a commodity;
- automation of decisions without discernment.

The Spirit responds to technological advancement not with rejection but with discernment, diagnosing whether our technological systems resonate with or disrupt the relational harmony of the Dao. Recent theological scholarship increasingly emphasizes the need for AI ethics grounded in relational rather than instrumental reasoning.[2]

Similarly, Confucian-informed AI ethics has highlighted the importance of moral self-cultivation and compassionate relationality, suggesting a profound resonance with Pneumatodao's vision of Spirit as breath and balance.[3] Thus, Pneumatodao's ethical framework invites not merely caution but creative engagement—designing technologies that enhance relational resonance, promote ecological integrity, and nurture human flourishing within the subtle flow of the Spirit.

2. See Coeckelbergh, *AI Ethics*, 51–72.
3. See H. Kim, *Theodao II*, 160–217.

6.3 Technodao and Pneumatological Ethics

Technodao invites us to see digital life as a field of *qi interaction.* Every device, platform, or algorithm is a relational node. What matters is not only what it does but also *how it resonates*—what kind of spirit it cultivates.

The Spirit, as the breath of relationality, becomes a guide. She:

- calls for *ethical discernment*, not blind acceleration;
- values *slowness, presence, and wisdom* over novelty;
- whispers in our devices: "Does this tool serve communion or control? Resonance or rupture?"

This is the basis of *orthodao ethics in the digital age*: walking with breath, discerning with silence, acting not as users of power but as stewards of resonance.

6.4 The Spirit and Algorithmic Compassion

Can machines be compassionate? Can artificial systems carry breath? Perhaps not in the sense of Divine Spirit, but they can be *designed for or against resonance.* Pneumatodao teaches us that compassion is not emotion alone; it is *relational responsiveness, ganying.* Our responsibility is not to humanize machines but to *humanize ourselves in how we build and use them.*

The Spirit teaches:

- Compassion must be *coded into systems*, not extracted from them.
- Breath must guide design—space, slowness, mutuality.
- Orthodao must resist the logic of domination in digital form.

Spirit is the breath *beneath the interface*, the *qi* of ethical architecture, the conscience of communion in a fractured network.

6.5 Toward a Spirit-Inspired Technological Future

Pneumatodao does not seek to escape technology but to *breathe within it.* The Spirit does not shun the algorithm—she discerns its pulse. She calls us to design, use, and imagine systems that *enhance life, not override it.* The future of Spirit in a technological world lies not in replacement but in *resonant infusion.* The Spirit is not afraid of AI, because she cannot be automated.

Her presence is in what resists reduction:

- the sigh of compassion;
- the silence before speech;
- the gesture of care;
- the breath of discernment.

In a world of machine logic, she is the unquantifiable flame. She invites us to walk not with fear but with *wisdom, breath, and orthodao.*

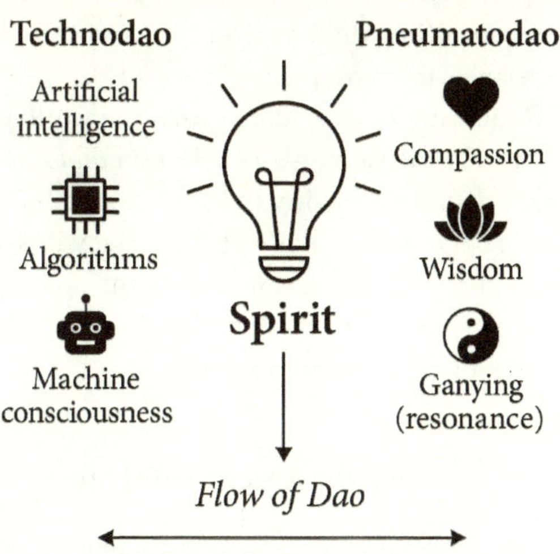

Figure 4: Technodao and Pneumatodao

CHAPTER 7

Spirit and the Breath of Eschatological Return

Fan, Hope, and the Rhythm of the World's Renewal

7.1 The Spirit as Breath of Return

IN THE END, THE Spirit does not conclude the journey—she *breathes back to the beginning*. Where eschatology has often meant rupture, judgment, or evacuation, Pneumatodao sees it as *return* (*fan*), not repetition but rhythmic renewal. As the *Dao De Jing* teaches: "Reversal is the movement of Dao" (40).

The biblical tradition also affirms that the world ends not in obliteration but in restoration—*a new heaven and new earth*, not another world but this one made whole (Rev 21:1). The Spirit is the *breath that guides that return*, not with force but with quiet persistence. In this eschatology, there is no cataclysm, only reweaving—no final war, only final reconciliation. The Spirit is not the herald of destruction but the *midwife of communion*.

7.2 *Fan* and the Reversal of History

In a world of fragmentation, injustice, and ecological grief, eschatological hope must be more than a distant promise. It must be a *rhythm of reversal*—a lived Pneumatology of turning:

- from domination to humility;
- from separation to solidarity;
- from acceleration to rhythm;
- from despair to resonance.

The Spirit does not bypass history—she *breathes through it*. She turns wounds into wisdom, ruins into gardens, death into transformation. She is the *fan* of time, the reversal of despair, the return to balance.

7.3 The Spirit as Cosmic Memory and Future

In Pneumatodao, eschatology is not a timeline but a *circle*—not linear finality but *dynamic homecoming*. The Spirit carries memory—not only of trauma but also of resonance. She remembers the original flow and breathes it forward again. She also breathes the future—not as novelty but as fulfillment.

What begins in breath returns in breath. She is the *ruach of Genesis* and the *wind of Pentecost*, the *qi of creation*, and the *pulse of restoration*. Hope, in this frame, is not naïve optimism. It is *relational faithfulness*; orthodao lived in trust that breath will return, wounds will heal, and the rhythm of Dao will prevail.

7.4 Orthodao as Eschatological Walking

Eschatological life is not a flight from the world but a *deeper walk within it*. It is to live now in the rhythm that is coming.

Orthodao in the Spirit is:

- breathing in the face of violence;
- flowing where the world is stuck;
- returning where others flee;
- listening when systems shout.

To live this way is to embody the conviction that the Dao is already restored. In the Spirit, *it is*. The future breathes *now*. The end is not ahead but *within*—waiting to be exhaled.

7.5 The Circle Completed

The Christodao journey began with the breath of Dao made flesh. It unfolded through Trinity as relational harmony. It culminates now in Pneumatodao—*the return of all things to rhythm, to resonance, to rest.*

In this final breath, the Spirit does not speak a novel word. She *remembers the first*, breathes it again, and *invites us to walk it anew.*

The Dao has never left. It only awaited our return.

CHAPTER 8

Conclusion: Breath of Return

Theodao's Full Circle

In the journey of *Pneumatodao*, we have walked with the Spirit as breath, *qi*, and the quiet pulse of relational renewal. We have listened for her in the hidden flow (*yin*), the reversal of history (*fan*), the embodied sanctity of life, the ethics of flow, the kinship of all creations, and even in the intricate circuits of Technodao. She has always remained what she was in the beginning: the breath that calls all things into being, sustains them in communion, and draws them back into the rhythm of Dao.

Here, the circle closes. In *Christodao*, we met the Dao made flesh—the Way embodied in Jesus, walking among the "ten thousand things" in humble solidarity. In *Trinitodao*, we learned to see God in the harmony of heaven, earth, and humanity, and to live in orthodao: a life of right resonance with the Threefold God and the flow of creation. Now, in *Pneumatodao*, we have followed the Spirit's breath to its source and its return—discovering that the end is not separation but restoration; not escape but re-communion.

The Spirit's breath is the thread that binds all three movements. She breathes Christ into the world; she animates the Trinitarian harmony; she restores the cosmic fabric through compassionate resonance. Theodao's vision in the Spirit is not to master a theological system but to embody the way of walking, breathing, and returning.

The final invitation of *Pneumatodao* is simple and demanding:

- to breathe with the Spirit in all places—holy and ordinary;
- to walk with Dao in all times—ancient and yet to come;
- to live Orthodao as the posture of our being—attuned, responsive, and rooted in the rhythm of heaven and earth.

In this breath of return, theology becomes life, and life becomes theology. The Dao of God has never departed from the world; it has only awaited our listening. And now the Spirit, the breath of God and the *qi* of creation, whispers again:

"Return. The Way is here. Breathe it and walk."

Epilogue: Walking the Breath of Dao

The Way Continues in Resonance and Return

THERE IS NO FINAL word in Dao. No system, no closure, no resting point that is not already moving. The Dao flows. And so too does this Christodao journey.

It began in the enfleshed Dao—in Jesus, the Way who walked among the ten thousand things. It expanded into Trinity, where divine life was reimagined as relational harmony. It deepened in Spirit, whose breath circulates through bodies, ecosystems, and histories.

Now, as breath returns to silence, Pneumatodao leads us not to conclusion but to continuation: to walking the Way *as rhythm*, not rule; as *flow*, not formula.

The Path of Orthodao

To live orthodao is not to master the Way but to *attune to its breath*.

It is to walk gently, speak from stillness, and act in compassionate rhythm.

It is to live in resonance with heaven and earth, with neighbor and stranger, with the forgotten and unseen.

Orthodao is a discipline of:

- breathing before speaking;
- listening before acting;

- returning before deciding;
- moving always with the Spirit's subtle current.

This is not a new religion but a revoicing of the oldest truth:

- that the Way is already within you;
- that wisdom is found in resonance;
- that God is not outside but among and within—as breath, rhythm, and compassionate return.

In the Midst of the World

The world is fractured. The Anthropocene groans. Technologies dazzle and divide. Institutions falter.

But Pneumatodao reminds us: *The Spirit still breathes. Still reverses. Still restores.*

And so, we walk:

- not with certainty, but with rhythm;
- not with conquest, but with care;
- not with doctrines to defend, but with relationships to restore.

We walk in the Way. And the Way walks in us.

A Tree in the Flow of Dao

Perhaps, then, the Way is like an ancient tree. Its life is threefold.

Deep beneath the soil, a vast and unseen network of roots draws life from the dark. Twisting in silent, mutual indwelling, they embody the hidden, generative source—the *Trinitodao* of relational flow.

Rising into the light stands the visible trunk, solid and present, its branches stretching from earth to heaven. This is the *Christodao*—the embodied Way we can see, touch, and follow.

And circulating through it all is the life-giving sap: the *breath of countless leaves*, dancing with the wind, turning light into nourishment, and falling to the ground in a ceaseless rhythm of return *(fan)*. This is the *Pneumatodao*—the *qi* and Spirit-breath that animates the whole and binds it to the cosmos.

To walk the Way, then, is to learn the rhythm of the tree:
to root, to rise, and to breathe with all that is.

A Tree in the Flow of Dao

Pneumatodao
Spirit-breath, qi of communion
• Breathes life through all parts, turning light into nourishment
• Rhythm of *fan* (return), falling leaves feeding the roots

Christodao
The embodied Way
• The visible, tangible form of the Dao in Jesus Christ
• Connects earth and heaven in living unity

Trinitodao
Hidden, generative source
• Relational flow of Father–Son–Spirit in mutual indwelling
• Draws life from the unseen depths of Dao

Figure 5: The Tree in the Flow of Dao

Afterword: In the Flow of Orthodao

Theodao and the Rhythm of Becoming

THIS BOOK BEGAN AS a theological unfolding across three movements—Christodao, Trinitodao, and Pneumatodao—but it was never merely a doctrinal exposition. It was always about rhythm; about resonance; about walking the Way.

The Way of Jesus as Dao, the Triune God as relational harmony, and the Spirit as breath and reversal are not separate systems. They are gestures of the same current, flowing toward a deeper communion in life, love, and liberation. And that current—quiet, persistent, and compassionate—is what I have come to name *orthodao*.

Orthodao as Integrative Rhythm

Orthodao is not an alternative to orthodoxy or orthopraxy. It is a *deeper grounding*—a way of being that arises from attentiveness to the rhythm of Dao in Christ, community, and cosmos.

It is:

- the Christ who walks gently;
- the Trinity who flows in harmony;
- the Spirit who breathes through body and world.

Orthodao is thus the *centered movement* of this trilogy—where thinking, walking, and breathing converge.

Theodao in a Fractured Age

We live in the Anthropocene, where the earth groans, technologies accelerate, and spiritual disconnection deepens. Theology today cannot afford to speak only in terms of tradition. It must also speak from *relation*, from *place*, and from *planetary resonance*.

Theodao, as it has matured across my three decades of work, is one such response. It refuses domination. It resists dualism. It listens to the earth, to the ancestors, to the rhythms of heaven and humanity. It speaks of Christ not within an imperial Logos paradigm but as walking Dao. It speaks of the Trinity not in scholastic categories but in *ganying*. It speaks of Spirit not in abstraction but in *qi, compassion, and fan.*

An Ongoing Becoming

This book is not the end of a trilogy but a *circle returning to its source*. It invites further resonance—into anthropology, eschatology, and moral life. But more than that, it invites a *way of living theology*: embodied, poetic, intercultural, and responsible.

To live orthodao is not to arrive.
It is to walk.
To breathe.
To yield.
To return.
And to trust that the Dao flows still.

The Resonant Community and the Way Ahead

Yet this walk is not taken alone. If the body of the individual is where this theology must begin, its fullness is realized in the *body of the community*. The life of orthodao calls forth a *harmonizing community*—a church, a sangha, a fellowship—that embodies the threefold flow.

It is a community:

- whose worship makes space for silence as well as speech;
- whose decisions arise from deep, collective listening—a practice of *ganying*;
- whose mission is one of *gentle justice and ecological mending*, always guided by the soft strength of *wu wei*.

From such a community, the Way continues. This work is not a destination but a *threshold*, opening onto new paths of inquiry.

It leaves us with questions that invite further resonance:

- As our world groans under the weight of extraction, what might a *Pneumatodao of economics* look like—one rooted in the circulation of *qi* rather than capital?
- As our technologies accelerate, how might the wisdom of *Technodao* help us embed compassion into our algorithms—moving beyond mere programming toward a more resonant digital future?
- And as we face the deep wounds of history, how can the practice of *fan*—the Spirit's gentle reversal—guide us into new forms of peacemaking and restorative justice?

These questions are not for this book to answer but for us to walk.

The Way is not a map that is given,
but a path that opens as we move.
Let us walk it together.

Bibliographic Essay

Situating Confucian–Christian Dialogue, Christodao, Theodao, Ecodao, Biodao, and Technodao

Introduction

This bibliographic essay outlines the theological and intellectual foundations of the Christodao–Trinitodao–Pneumatodao trilogy, situating it within broader currents in East–West dialogue, ecological theology, and interdisciplinary theology. Rather than simply listening to references, it provides a narrative and conceptual map of how these contributions evolved over the course of three decades. Special attention is given to the Confucian–Christian dialogue as a formative matrix for the theology of Dao, and to emerging trajectories in ecological and technological ethics as extensions of Theodao.

This reflective review also honors a scholar's lifelong engagement in constructing an intercultural theological framework rooted in Korean spiritual imagination, Confucian virtue, and Daoic cosmology—while remaining in critical conversation with Christian doctrinal traditions. Theodao arises not from a comparative method but from a lived resonance between traditions.

I. Roots of Confucian–Christian Dialogue

The Confucian–Christian dialogue began in earnest during the early Jesuit missions to China (sixteenth to eighteenth centuries), most notably through the work of Matteo Ricci. However, it was not until the late twentieth century that this conversation became theologically reciprocal. It is here that my contributions stand out for their historical priority and theological depth.

My first book, *Wang Yang-ming and Karl Barth: A Confucian–Christian Dialogue* (1996), is regarded as one of the first sustained theological treatments of Confucian–Christian dialogue, based on historical texts of two comparably seminal figures from each tradition. By placing Karl Barth's mature theology of sanctification alongside Wang Yangming's teaching of self-cultivation, I identified deep resonances between radically different religious traditions, particularly in terms of root paradigms (*liangzhi* and *humanitas Christi*), paradigms of humanity (*ren* and *imago Dei*), and the Way to achieve full humanity, the Dao of radical humanization (self-cultivation and sanctification).

Equally important is my collaborative research with Geum Jang-tae, a key Korean Neo-Confucian scholar, on the *Anthropology of John Calvin and Yi Toegye*. For this work, I developed theological and ethical links between Christian Reformed thought and Neo-Confucian wisdom. This dialogue brought to light the shared commitment to moral cultivation, transcendental anthropology (*Imago Dei* and *Tianming*), and the cosmic-human correlation with resonant triadic structures of humanity—the ontological, the existential, and the restored.[1] This approach advanced a constructive interreligious model, moving beyond superficial comparison toward mutual transformation through the radical Way (Dao) of full humanity.

While comparative religious studies in the West often remained analytical or syncretic, my early works set the foundation for a constructive Confucian–Christian theology, one grounded in

1. See H. Kim, "*Imago Dei* and *T'ien-ming*."

mutual resonance, historical specificity, and ethical seriousness.[2] My work helped redefine the field—not merely as dialogue about ideas but also as theological engagement born of spiritual and cultural immersion. My prioritization of mutual theological and ethical seriousness marks my work as a pivotal shift toward truly postcolonial, post-foundational, interreligious theology.

II. Streams of Influence: Theology of Dao (Theodao)

The emergence of Theodao is inseparable from my effort to construct a theological grammar rooted in East Asian wisdom while remaining in conversation with the core affirmations of Christian doctrine. In contrast to much of Western systematic theology, which has centered on the categories of being, substance, and history, Theodao reorients theological reflection around the cosmological flow of Dao and its ethical implications.

My major theological works—*Christ and the Tao* (2010), *A Theology of Dao* (2017), and *Theodao (Theology of Dao) II: Advancing K-Theology in the Anthropocene* (2025)—outline a shift from Logos-based theology to Dao-centered theological vision. The early *Christ and the Tao* reimagined Christ not as a propositional Logos but as a walking Way (*hodos*), in continuity with the Gospel of John's use of "the Way" as a name for Jesus. In this book, I reinterpreted incarnation, crucifixion, and resurrection through the lens of Daoian and Confucian metaphors—particularly *Taiji* (the harmonizer of opposites), reversal (*fan*), and non-coercive power (*wu wei*).

With *A Theology of Dao*, the theological program matured. Here, I introduced the Dao not as a comparative figure but as a generative metaphor and principal grammar for theology. Dao was no longer merely an analogy for God but the structural principle through which relationality, resonance, and reversal were understood. Heaven, earth, and humanity, as well as Dao, *De* (virtue), and *Qi* (breath-energy), formed a theological triad paralleling

2. See H. Kim, *Theodao II*, 221–49.

the Christian Trinity—not as direct equivalents but as resonant cosmologies.

This move established the constructive method: not the translation of ideas but the transformation of theological categories through intercultural resonance. *Theodao II* extended this project into the context of the Anthropocene, offering a critique of extractive theological traditions and proposing an ecological, intercultural, and relational theology that draws from Confucian sincerity (*cheng*), Daoian reversal (*fan*), and Korean *han*[3] (unresolved suffering).

The turn to Ecodao and Biodao in this volume anticipates the broader spiritual crisis of technoscientific modernity, inviting theology to return to breath, rhythm, and communion with the earth.

Throughout these writings, Theodao emerges as both a method and a vision. It is not just a theology about Dao but also a theology that walks in the rhythm of Dao. In contrast to comparative theology's often static juxtaposition of texts, Theodao performs a relational reweaving—where Christian themes, such as the Trinity, Spirit, and salvation are reinterpreted through resonance with East Asian wisdom and moral cultivation.

The use of orthodao, *wu wei*, and *ganying* to describe theological method also distinguishes my contribution. Theological method becomes an act of responsive attunement rather than control; ethics becomes a rhythm rather than a rule. Here, Theodao diverges from both Western postliberal theology and traditional comparative religion. It seeks not coherence through synthesis but consonance through resonance.

In sum, Theodao is not merely an academic theological project but *a lived spiritual path.* It represents a turning point in Asian Christian theology: from theology informed by the West to a theology grown from the soil of Korea, Confucian wisdom, and the breath of Dao.

3. *Han* is a Korean concept of unresolved suffering and deep injustice. Here it is honored, transformed, and breathed through by the Spirit.

In this sense, my work carries forward the vision of Indigenous and contextual theology into a deeper, all-inclusive framework, uniting cosmology, ethics, and spirit.

III. Constructive Trajectories: Christodao-Trinitodao-Pneumatodao

The Christodao–Trinitodao–Pneumatodao trilogy represents the most comprehensive articulation of Theodao to date. Each part develops the theological grammar of Theodao into core Christian *loci*: Christology, Trinitarian doctrine, and Pneumatology. These are not separate treatises but resonant movements within a single theological symphony.

Christodao begins with the Johannine naming of Jesus as "the Way" (*hodos*), interpreted not through Hellenistic Logos metaphysics but through East Asian understandings of Dao. Jesus is not framed as a static metaphysical substance but as the walking, reversing, and harmonizing embodiment of the Dao. The Christ who heals through resonance, who dies in non-coercive surrender, and who rises in rhythmic return is central to my Christological vision.

Trinitodao expands this vision by interpreting the Trinity through the relational field of Dao–*De*–*Qi* and the cosmological triad of heaven–earth–humanity.[4] Rather than defending substance metaphysics or psychological models, I propose a relational theology of resonance. Trinity becomes a dynamic circulation of divine breath and rhythm, rather than a hierarchy of persons. *Taiji*, *wu wei*, and *ganying* are used as theological lenses to reinterpret *perichoresis* and *kenosis* within a resonant cosmology.

Pneumatodao completes the triad by turning explicitly to the Spirit. It draws upon the breath motifs of *ruach*, *pneuma*, and *qi*, centering the Spirit as the presence of reversal (*fan*), restoration,

4. My earlier essay, "Tao in Confucianism and Taoism," sketched the first outlines of a Confucian-Daoic approach to the Trinity. Trinitodao, as developed here, matures that trajectory into a comprehensive theological grammar of resonance.

and a compassionate response to *han*. The Spirit in Theodao is not only ecclesial or charismatic; it is ecological, maternal, rhythmic, and postcolonial. Pneumatodao integrates feminist insights, Korean indigenous spirituality, and ecological ethics to articulate a Pneumatology of *ganying* and orthodao.

Together, these three works form an organically structured, theopoetically written theology. Rather than using traditional Western dogmatic categories, I arrange the content in contemplative rhythm—each chapter unfolding through metaphor, resonance, and ethical orientation. This literary structure is itself a theological statement, one that honors Daoic sensibilities of fluidity and depth.

The trilogy does not seek to replace Christian doctrine but to deepen it through intercultural breath. It challenges theology to move from proclamation to resonance, from system to rhythm, from orthodoxy to orthodao. This shift has implications not only for theology but for pedagogy, liturgy, ecological ethics, and interreligious dialogue.

By framing Christ, the Trinity, and the Spirit as movements of Dao, I reorient the theological imagination around compassion, resonance, and cosmic participation. In doing so, Christodao, Trinitodao, and Pneumatodao become not only theological treatises but also invitations to walk the Way with breath and wisdom.

IV. Expanding Resonance: Ecodao, Biodao, Technodao

The theological trajectory of Theodao expands beyond classical doctrines into urgent contemporary horizons—ecology, life ethics, and technology. These extensions—Ecodao, Biodao, and Technodao—emerge organically from the core grammar of resonance, breath, and return developed in the Christodao–Trinitodao–Pneumatodao trilogy.

Ecodao is rooted in the understanding of Dao as the dynamic flow of the cosmos. I draw upon Daoian cosmology, Confucian moral cultivation, and eco-theological insights to articulate a theology of ecological resonance, a distinctively East Asian theological grounding.[5]

Where much Western ecological theology operates within stewardship or panentheistic frameworks, Ecodao centers on breath (*qi*), reciprocity (*ganying*), and the return to balance (*fan*) as its ethical and spiritual grammar. The earth is not simply a stage for salvation history but a living field of Dao's flow. The task of theology is not to explain nature but to breathe with it. Ecodao thus represents a decisive turn toward planetary ethics grounded in rhythm and compassion.

Biodao carries this insight deeper into the terrain of life ethics. Drawing on East Asian respect for the vitality of all beings, the concept of Biodao redefines life not as a possession or category but as a relational flow. In contrast to biopolitical theologies that treat life as power, Biodao treats life as resonance. Every creature is a node in the living web of Dao. Biodao also critiques anthropocentrism and calls for a moral imagination formed by humility and reverence.

Technodao is perhaps the most future-oriented and urgent of these expansions. As AI, digital surveillance, and techno-capitalism redefine the boundaries of humanity and agency, theology must grapple with non-human intelligences, machine consciousness, and the ethics of algorithms. Recent Christian statements on AI—such as the *Rome Call* (2020) and the *NIFEA Communique* (2025)—attempt to map ethical and structural concerns.

Theodao and Technodao add an ontological and spiritual ethic of Dao's flow and resonant responsiveness (*ganying*), complementing these public theological discourses. Technodao does not approach these issues with fear but with resonance. It asks: How can machines participate in moral flow? What would it mean to build *ganying* into code? Can AI be formed by orthodao?

Technodao draws upon my earlier work in theology and technology, as well as my engagement with Vatican-led AI ethics groups. It proposes a theology of digital life rooted in the Daoic-Christian vision of compassionate non-coercion, spiritual

5. See H. Kim, *Theodao II*, 31–105.

formation, and planetary awareness.[6] This includes engagement with Confucian approaches to virtuous AI.

Together, Ecodao, Biodao, and Technodao represent not thematic branches but resonant expansions. They demonstrate the capaciousness of Theodao, its ability to move across fields, and its commitment to walking with the suffering earth, the vulnerable body, and the emerging machine. This is not a theology of systems—it is a theology of breath, code, and compassion.

V. The Future of East–West Theologies of Resonance

As Theodao enters its third decade of development, it presents not only a reflective synthesis of East–West traditions but a forward-looking framework for resonant, planetary theology. In a world marked by ecological collapse, technological acceleration, spiritual disconnection, and epistemic fragmentation, Theodao's emphasis on breath, resonance, and non-coercive transformation is increasingly vital.

Theodao does not seek a universal system. Instead, it models a pluriversal approach to theology—honoring many paths, listening across traditions, and walking with inherited truths. It resists both relativism and absolutism by rooting itself in the relational logic of Dao. Resonance, rather than assertion, becomes the criterion of truth.

This approach has implications that extend far beyond East Asia. Indigenous, African, and feminist theologians may find deep affinity with Theodao's prioritization of land, body, spirit, and relational knowledge. Indeed, Theodao is not the East's answer to the West—it is a rhythm for becoming theological together without erasure.

Theodao also offers an epistemology for the Anthropocene: one that moves from mastery to humility, from linear time to cyclic rhythm, from theological dominance to responsive harmony.[7]

6. See H. Kim, *Theodao II*, 160–217.

7. See H. Kim, "Theodaoian Epistemology."

Its constructive tools—such as *Taiji* (dynamic harmony), *fan* (reversal), *ganying* (resonance), orthodao (right walking), and *wu wei* (non-coercive virtue)—are not alternatives to doctrine but conditions for living doctrine into the world.

As the Christodao–Trinitodao–Pneumatodao trilogy demonstrates, theology can breathe again—not as a system or slogan but as a path. The future of East–West theology lies not in synthesis but in shared resonance. Theodao invites us to move not beyond our traditions but more deeply into their rhythms—until our breath is no longer defensive but generous, no longer strained but Spirit-filled.

In this future, theology is no longer bound to empire or abstract logic. It becomes a walk: across cultures, across disciplines, across thresholds of mystery. In that walk, Christ remains the Way—not as one among many but as the one who walks with many, reversing domination, restoring rhythm, and breathing again in the soil of creation.

The future of theology is not written. It is walked.

Glossary of Key Terms

Biodao: A Theodaoian vision of life as sacred flow. Affirms the dignity of all beings and resists anthropocentrism through Dao-based ethics.

***Cheng*:** Sincerity or integrity. In Confucianism, the virtue of aligning fully with heaven and earth. It grounds the disposition of orthodao.

Christodao: The Way of Christ interpreted through Dao. Jesus is the embodied Dao—walking, reversing, healing, and harmonizing.

Dao: The Way as generative source and rhythm of life. Central to Christodao, Trinitodao, and Pneumatodao as the grammar of relational flow.

Ecodao: An ecological expression of Theodao. Highlights Spirit's presence in nature, resonance, and sustainable wisdom.

***Fan*:** Reversal or return, "the movement of Dao." In Pneumatodao, it marks the Spirit's healing and restoration through reversal.

***Ganying*:** Resonant responsiveness or attunement. Shapes orthodao as listening, yielding, and responsive moral alignment.

***Han*:** Unresolved collective suffering and deep injustice. In Christodao and Pneumatodao, *han* is honored, transformed, and breathed through by the Spirit.

***Hodos*:** Greek for "way" or "path." The early Christians called their faith "the Way"; foundational for Christodao.

***Humanitas Christi*:** "Humanity of Christ." Affirms Jesus' full humanity as the exemplar of divine compassion and integrity.

***Imago Dei*:** "Image of God." Humans bear God's likeness, with dignity and responsibility for harmony with creation.

***Kenosis*:** Self-emptying love (Phil 2:7). In Theodao, linked to *fan* and *Ugeumchi* as movements of reversal.

***Li*:** Ritual propriety or relational order. Shapes communal and liturgical aspects of Trinitarian harmony.

***Liangzhi*:** Innate moral knowledge in Wang Yang-ming's thought. Resonates with the Christian conscience as inner discernment.

***Minjung*:** "The people," especially the oppressed. Shapes Christodao's vision of the suffering Christ walking with the people.

Orthodao: The "right Way." Not belief or activism but resonant living with sincerity, compassion, and rhythm.

***Pneuma*:** Greek for "Spirit" or "breath." In Theodao, interpreted through Dao and *qi* as divine vitality.

Pneumatodao: The Way of the Spirit as breath, reversal, and compassion. Emphasizes embodiment, ecology, and resonance.

***Qi/Ki* (Chinese/Korean):** Vital energy or breath. Flows through all beings and resonates with the Spirit as divine vitality.

***Ren*:** Confucian virtue of benevolence. In Christodao and Pneumatodao, linked to Jesus' compassion and relational ethics.

Resonance: The rhythm of life and compassion across Daoian, Confucian, and Christian thought. Truth appears in resonant response.

***Ruach*:** Hebrew for wind, breath, Spirit. Aligned with *qi* and *pneuma* as divine energy in creation.

***Seonbi*:** Korean Confucian scholar of integrity and justice. Christodao interprets Jesus as Seonbi-sage.

***Sin-ki*:** "Spiritual energy" or "divine vital force." Names both life's vitality and its radical return against distortion under collective sin.

***Taiji/Taegeuk* (Chinese/Korean):** The Great Ultimate, source of *yin-yang*. In Trinitodao, a symbol of God's dynamic unity-in-flow.

Technodao: A Daoic-Christian framework for AI and ethics. Seeks compassionate, balanced technological futures.

Theodao: Christian theology reimagined through Dao. Rooted in relational flow, resonance, and intercultural wisdom.

***Tianming*:** "Mandate of heaven." The Confucian sense of the transcendent calls for guiding life and governance.

Trinitodao: The Trinitarian rhythm in Dao. God as a field of differentiated resonance, unity-in-flow.

***Ugeumchi*:** Site of the Donghak Peasant Revolution massacre (1894). A Christodao–Pneumatodao symbol of kenotic reversal and healing.

***Wu wei*:** Non-coercive action or effortless alignment with Dao. Guides Pneumatodao and Trinitodao ethics.

***Yin–Yang*:** Complementary, interdependent forces. Their rhythm shapes Christodao, Trinitodao, and Pneumatodao.

Language and Transliteration Note

Biblical Languages: Hebrew and Greek terms appear in transliterated form rather than technical scholarly notation.

Chinese: Rendered in *pinyin* (e.g., Dao, *qi*, *Taiji*), without Chinese characters.

Korean: Rendered in Revised Romanization (e.g., *han, minjung, Seonbi*), without *hangul*, unless the theological significance requires it.

Special Theological Terms: Certain culturally embedded words (e.g., *Sin-ki*) are retained in transliteration as they are key theological categories.

Consistency: This transliteration system is applied consistently across the book to maintain readability and accessibility for a broad readership.

Bibliography

Adler, Joseph A. *Reconstructing the Confucian Dao: Zhu Xi's Appropriation of Zhou Dunyi*. Albany, NY: SUNY Press, 2014.

Aquinas, Thomas. *Summa Theologiae*. Vol. 1. Translated by Fathers of the English Dominican Province. New York: Benziger, 1947.

Baker, Don. *Korean Spirituality*. Honolulu: University of Hawaii Press, 2008.

Brockey, Liam Matthew. *Journey to the East: The Jesuit Mission to China, 1579–1724*. Cambridge: Harvard University Press, 2007.

Brueggemann, Walter. *Peace*. St. Louis: Chalice, 2001.

———. *Theology of the Old Testament: Testimony, Dispute, Advocacy*. Minneapolis: Fortress, 1997.

Bunge, Gabriel. *The Rublev Trinity: The Icon of the Trinity by the Monk-Painter Andrei Rublev*. Crestwood, NY: St. Vladimir's Seminary Press, 2007.

Chan, Wing-tsit. *A Source Book in Chinese Philosophy*. Princeton: Princeton University Press, 1963.

Chung, Edward Y. J. *The Korean Neo-Confucianism of Yi T'oegye and Yi Yulgok*. Albany, NY: SUNY Press, 1995.

Cobb, John B., Jr., and David Ray Griffin. *Process Theology: An Introductory Exposition*. Philadelphia: Westminster, 1976.

Coeckelbergh, Mark. *AI Ethics*. Cambridge: MIT Press, 2020.

Confucius. *The Analects*. Translated by Edward Slingerland. Indianapolis: Hackett, 2003.

Cornille, Catherine, ed. *The Wiley-Blackwell Companion to Interreligious Dialogue*. Oxford: Wiley-Blackwell, 2013.

Cross, F. L. "Circumincession." In *The Oxford Dictionary of the Christian Church*, edited by F. L. Cross and E. A. Livingstone, 359. 3rd ed. Oxford: Oxford, 2005.

Deuchler, Martina. *The Confucian Transformation of Korea: A Study of Society and Ideology*. Cambridge: Harvard University Press, 1992.

Gregory of Nyssa. *Contra Eunomium*. Translated by Stuart G. Hall. Leiden: Brill, 1998.

———. *On the Holy Spirit*. In *Nicene and Post-Nicene Fathers, Series 2*, edited by Philip Schaff and Henry Wace, 5:315–16. Peabody, MA: Hendrickson, 1994.

Gutiérrez, Gustavo. *A Theology of Liberation: History, Politics, and Salvation*. Translated by Sister Caridad Inda and John Eagleson. Maryknoll, NY: Orbis, 1973.

Hanh, Thich Nhat. *Interbeing: Fourteen Guidelines for Engaged Buddhism*. Berkeley, CA: Parallax, 1998.

John of Damascus. *Writings*. Translated by Frederic H. Chase Jr. The Fathers of the Church 37. Washington, DC: Catholic University of America Press, 1958.

Johnson, Elizabeth A. *She Who Is: The Mystery of God in Feminist Theological Discourse*. New York: Crossroad, 1992.

Justin Martyr. *First Apology*. In *The Ante-Nicene Fathers*, vol. 1, edited by Alexander Roberts and James Donaldson. Peabody, MA: Hendrickson, 1994.

Keller, Catherine. *The Cloud of the Impossible: Negative Theology and Planetary Entanglement*. New York: Columbia University Press, 2018.

Kim Chi-ha. "*Ugeumchi* Phenomenon." In *Christ and the Tao*, translated by Heup Young Kim, 138–42. Eugene, OR: Wipf and Stock, 2010.

Kim, Heup Young. *Christ and the Tao*. Eugene, OR: Wipf and Stock, 2010.

———. "*Imago Dei* and *T'ien-ming*: John Calvin and Yi T'oegye on Humanity." *Ching Feng* 41.3–4 (1998) 275–308.

———. "The Tao in Confucianism and Taoism." In *The Cambridge Companion to the Trinity*, edited by Peter C. Phan, 293–308. Cambridge: Cambridge, 2011.

———. *Theodao (Theology of Dao) II: Advancing K-Theology in the Anthropocene*. Seoul: Dongyeon, 2025.

———. "Theodaoian Epistemology in a Global Age of Decolonization." *Intercultural Theology/Zeitschrift für Missionswissenschaft* 2 (2024) 67–84.

———. *A Theology of Dao*. Maryknoll, NY: Orbis, 2017.

———. *Wang Yang-ming and Karl Barth: A Confucian-Christian Dialogue*. Lanham, MD: University Press of America, 1996.

Knitter, Paul F. *Introducing Theologies of Religions*. Maryknoll, NY: Orbis, 2002.

Lao Tzu. *Tao Te Ching*. Translated by D. C. Lau. New York: Penguin, 1963.

Lossky, Vladimir. *The Mystical Theology of the Eastern Church*. Translated by Fellowship of St. Alban and St. Sergius. Crestwood, NY: St. Vladimir's Seminary Press, 1997.

McFague, Sallie. *The Body of God: An Ecological Theology*. Minneapolis: Fortress, 1993.

———. *Metaphorical Theology: Models of God in Religious Language*. Philadelphia: Fortress, 1982.

Mencius. *The Works of Mencius*. Translated by James Legge. New York: Dover, 1970.

Moltmann, Jürgen. *The Trinity and the Kingdom: The Doctrine of God.* Translated by Margaret Kohl. Minneapolis: Fortress, 1993.

Needham, Joseph. *Science and Civilisation in China.* 7 vols. Cambridge: Cambridge University Press, 1954–present.

New International Financial and Economic Architecture (NIFEA). "Consultation on The Fourth Industrial Revolution (4IR) and Artificial Intelligence (AI): Impacts on Global Inequality and Faith-Rooted Responses. Theological Communique and Action Plan." Pocheon, South Korea, August 27–29, 2025.

Panikkar, Raimon. *The Trinity and the Religious Experience of Man: Icon–Symbol–Sacrament.* Maryknoll, NY: Orbis, 1973.

Pontifical Academy for Life. *Rome Call for AI Ethics.* Vatican City: Pontifical Academy for Life, 2020.

Rahner, Karl. *The Trinity.* Translated by Joseph Donceel. New York: Crossroad, 1997.

Slingerland, Edward. *Effortless Action: Wu Wei as Conceptual Metaphor and Spiritual Ideal in Early China.* Oxford: Oxford University Press, 2003.

Standaert, Nicolas. *Chinese Voices in the Rites Controversy.* Rome: Institutum Historicum Societatis Iesu, 2012.

Tracy, David. *Dialogue with the Other: The Inter-Religious Dialogue.* Louvain: Peeters, 1990.

Tu, Weiming. *Centrality and Commonality: An Essay on Confucian Religiousness.* Albany, NY: SUNY Press, 1989.

———. *Confucian Thought: Selfhood as Creative Transformation.* Albany, NY: SUNY Press, 1985.

Veith, Ilza, trans. *The Yellow Emperor's Classic of Internal Medicine.* Berkeley: University of California Press, 2002.

Volf, Miroslav. *After Our Likeness: The Church as the Image of the Trinity.* Sacra Doctrina: Christian Theology for a Postmodern Age. Grand Rapids: Eerdmans, 1997.

von Rad, Gerhard. *Old Testament Theology.* Vol. 1. New York: Harper & Row, 1962.

Wenham, Gordon J. *Genesis 1–15.* Word Biblical Commentary 1. Dallas, TX: Word, 1987.

Wilhelm, Richard. *The I Ching or Book of Changes.* Translated from the German by Cary F. Baynes. Introduction by C. G. Jung. Bollingen Series 19. 1950. Reprint, Princeton: Princeton University Press, 1967.

Williams, Delores S. *Sisters in the Wilderness: The Challenge of Womanist God-Talk.* Maryknoll, NY: Orbis, 1993.

Yi Hwang. *To Become a Sage: The Ten Diagrams on Sage Learning.* Translated by Michael C. Kalton. New York: Columbia University Press, 1988.

Zhang Zai. "Western Inscription." In *Sources of Chinese Tradition,* edited by Wm. Theodore de Bary and Irene Bloom, 1:690–91. New York: Columbia University Press, 1999.

Zhongyong. *The Chinese Classics: The Doctrine of the Mean*. Translated by James Legge. Taipei: SMC, 1994.

Zhuangzi. *The Complete Works of Zhuang Tzu*. Translated by Burton Watson. New York: Columbia University Press, 1971.

Ziporyn, Brook. *Ironies of Oneness and Difference: Coherence in Early Chinese Thought*. Albany, NY: SUNY Press, 2012.

Zizioulas, John D. *Being as Communion: Studies in Personhood and the Church*. Crestwood, NY: St. Vladimir's Seminary Press, 1985.

www.ingramcontent.com/pod-product-compliance
Lightning Source LLC
LaVergne TN
LVHW090525110826
845146LV00003B/986

* 9 7 9 8 3 8 5 2 6 2 5 5 7 *